WHAT HAPPENED TO THE FIRE?

WHAT HAPPENED TO THE FIRE?

Rekindling the Blaze of Charismatic Renewal

J. Lee Grady

Chosen Books

A Division of Baker Book House
Grand Rapids, Michigan 49516

Published by Chosen Books
a division of Baker Book House Company
P.O. Box 6287, Grand Rapids, MI 49516–6287

Printed in the United States of America

Library of Congress Cataloging-in-Publication Data

Grady, J. Lee
    What happened to the fire? : rekindling the blaze of charismatic
renewal / J. Lee Grady
      p. cm.
   ISBN 0-8007-9212-2
    1. Pentecostalism. 2. Pentecostal churches. 3. Church renewal—
Pentecostal churches. 4. Grady, J. Lee. I. Title.
   BR1644.G73   1944
   270.8′2—dc20   93-40052

SPECIAL THANKS

To my parents, Jack and Jean Grady, who taught me to trust the Lord.

To Barry St. Clair, who challenged me to surrender to the Lordship of Jesus.

To June Leverette, who introduced me to the Person and work of the Holy Spirit.

To my wife, Deborah, who inspires me to live a life of faithfulness to God.

Contents

Preface

uban pastor Emilio Gonzales had never heard of the term *baptism in the Holy Spirit* until one Sunday in the mid–1950s, when a Methodist bishop from Mexico visited the Vedado Methodist Church in downtown Havana. The old bishop asked everyone in the congregation to kneel and pray for God's Spirit to empower them, and Emilio, who was just entering the ministry at the time, followed instructions eagerly.

What followed was Emilio's personal version of Pentecost. He described his experience to me in the fall of 1993, when I visited Havana to investigate how churches had been faring since Fidel Castro relaxed restrictions on religion in Cuba.

A frail man with a gentle smile, Emilio told me in vivid detail about his first encounter with the Baptizer.

"I began to feel an electric current go from my head to my feet," he said. "I lifted my hands and began crying and laughing. I felt I had been bathed in God's presence."

After this unusual event, the Mexican bishop left town. Emilio had no one with whom to compare his experience and no access to books about the Holy Spirit. All he had was his Bible.

"I had to judge for myself," he told me. "I examined everything very carefully. No one else understood it."

Though it seemed like an insignificant moment, what happened that day at the Vedado Church would dramatically alter Cuba's spiritual climate. A fire was ignited that would spread quietly throughout the island—a fire that would prove to be unquenchable, even in a country in which Christian belief was discouraged and pastors were routinely banished to prison camps.

Over the next few years, following Cuba's 1959 revolution, many of the Methodist pastors who did not flee their homeland were "strangely warmed" by the same fire that burned in Emilio's heart. Rinaldo Gonzales, a young seminarian studying at a Methodist school in the city of Matanzas, discovered this heaven-sent fire in 1979 when a visiting professor from the United States told students at a chapel service that she had been baptized in the Holy Spirit. Rinaldo, his wife and some other students prayed for an infilling of God's power and began speaking in tongues.

A few months later, before he could finish his studies, Rinaldo was labeled a criminal by the Cuban government and sent to a labor camp. But the fire he encountered at the seminary in Matanzas only burned more brightly during those dark days he spent away from his wife and infant daughter. The Holy Spirit's presence renewed and invigorated him, and confirmed to him that God had called him to share Christ with his countrymen.

When I met Rinaldo in 1993, he was pastoring a lively congregation of young people—many of them new converts—at the same Vedado Church where Emilio Gonzales had been baptized in the Spirit forty years earlier. The Communists were not interfering with the work of the church, and the young people worshiped without fear of recrimination.

"We are not praying for a revival," Rinaldo told me. "We are in a revival. There is a growing church in Cuba, a powerful and dynamic church. This movement is quiet, but strong."

Like the majority of Methodist churches in Cuba, Rinaldo's congregation is fully charismatic in doctrine and worship style. On a typical Wednesday night at the Vedado Church, the young members clap, shake tambourines and raise their hands as they sing lively praise choruses. Some of them stood in front of the congregation and shared words of prophecy and exhortation.

Just east of Havana at the Methodist Church of Marianao, where Emilio Gonzales was pastoring a large congregation, the same charismatic format was evident when I stopped in for a visit.

Charismatic renewal has transformed an entire denomination in Cuba—a denomination not known for the same kind of evangelical fervor in the United States. According to Rinaldo, an estimated 75 percent of Methodist pastors in his country consider themselves charismatic or Pentecostal. It is possible that the entire Methodist denomination in Cuba could be in renewal within a few years.

How did this happen? As renewal fires spread during the 1970s and '80s, churches began to evangelize in spite of government intimidation. After Castro aired a landmark apology in 1990 for discriminating against Christians, the Methodists started one hundred new churches in three years. Other Pentecostal groups, like the Assemblies of God and the Pentecostal Holiness Church, were also growing at impressive rates, as more and more Cubans realized they were free to believe.

One night during my visit to Cuba, I drove with Rinaldo to observe what he called a house church located in the Havana suburb of Cojimar. As we drove past crumbling buildings and austere Communist monuments, I imagined that the meeting would take place in a tiny living room with a dozen people. When we arrived, I was surprised to find 125 believers of all ages jammed into the front yard of a modest concrete block home. The worshipers, all of whom had walked or ridden bicycles to get to the church service, were singing when we arrived. Their praises could be heard all over the neighborhood, but no one seemed to mind.

As I took my seat on a cold stone step and began to clap along, I was struck by how joyful these Cuban believers were. Their voices were exuberant, their eyes glowed with radiance and their bright smiles made up for the fact that a power shortage had forced them to meet in total darkness—except for a single kerosene lantern that was hanging crudely on a wire by the front porch.

As we began to sing a reverent worship song in Spanish, most people closed their eyes and lifted their hands toward heaven. A few shed tears as they praised God for His love and mercy. But I could not close my eyes. I was too busy looking around at the remarkable scene.

How can these people be so happy? I thought to myself. I knew the kinds of conditions they lived in. I knew they had eaten very little that day, except for maybe some rice or bread. I knew that life in Cuba was marked by hardship and pain. Yet these Christians seemed to be living in a realm of faith that was as foreign to me as their language and customs.

After we finished singing, several people stood to give testimonies about how God had helped them walk through the trials of the week. One young woman said that she had been converted because some women from the church visited her in the hospital and prayed for her healing. God delivered her of cancer, she said, adding that she went home and destroyed her Santeria idols and other occult fetishes. Later, in his lengthy sermon, Rinaldo used the woman's story to illustrate that God wants to perform miracles today just as He did during Jesus' earthly ministry.

When we closed the service with more singing, I studied the scene again in amazement, tears filling my eyes. Never in my life had I witnessed a more genuine expression of Christianity. *This must be what the New Testament Church was like,* I thought.

When I returned to my hotel room, from which I could look out over the city of Havana, I pondered what God had been doing on that isolated island over the past forty years. In spite of scarcity, Marxist control, officially sanctioned atheism and total isolation from the United States, the fire of God's Spirit has been sweeping the country. The blaze of spiritual renewal that began in the 1950s has proven more powerful than Castro's regime. It will outlive Marxism in Cuba.

Before I left Havana, I sat down with Rinaldo Hernandez and the bishop of the Methodist Church of Cuba, Joel Ajo. We talked about the revival and about the needs of the churches there: training for ministers, youth ministry materials, Sunday school literature and, most of all, simple encouragement. Eager to take advantage of new opportunities to minister in Cuba, the bishop extended a warm invitation to American church groups to visit his country.

Suddenly I felt disturbed. I wanted American Christians to see for themselves how the Spirit was transforming the churches of Cuba, but it pained me to think that we might infect Cuban congregations with the same disease that has quenched and snuffed out the fires of revival in our own country.

These Cuban church leaders have more to offer us in the United States, it seemed to me, that than we can possibly offer them. Perhaps it would be better for Cuban pastors to come to America, I thought, and teach us what the Holy Spirit has taught them.

I breathed a prayer of desperation as I imagined a worse-case scenario: *Lord, don't let us charismatics bring our money-centered gospel to these starving people. Don't let us mislead these precious saints with our own misguided doctrines. And most of all, Lord, don't let us duplicate our denominational divisions here in a place where every believer needs the support of the entire Body of Christ.*

As I boarded my plane at José Martí Airport in Havana and returned to Miami, I thought much about the state of the churches in my country. I was haunted by one question: What happened to the fire in America's churches? Thousands of pastors in America have been "strangely warmed" by the same Holy Spirit who impacted men like Emilio Gonzales and Rinaldo Hernandez. Hundreds of thousands of charismatic churches have been started in the United States since the early 1970s. Yet church growth has stagnated in recent years. In most American churches, the fire of Pentecost is no longer blazing.

If Cuba's churches were languishing today, their leaders could easily blame their condition on a lack of resources. It has only been since 1990, after all, that Bibles became available there in government-run stores. But the spiritual coldness that exists in American churches cannot be blamed on a lack of resources. We publish more Bibles, hymnals, Christian books and church literature than any other nation on earth, and we use most of what we publish within our own borders. We spend millions of dollars on church buildings and denominational facilities. We have conferences on every imaginable topic, and we offer programs designed to cure every spiritual problem. But our churches are not on fire for God.

Why does spiritual revival seem so elusive to us?

I have pondered that question for several years, since I was once part of a revival movement that collapsed because of human weaknesses. Although I believe that God sovereignly gives revival, I also believe that revival cannot occur unless God's people are committed to following not their own agenda but the agenda of the Holy Spirit. Too many times in this century, movements that were born of the Spirit ended up as spiritual miscarriages. And in every case, men and women were responsible for derailing God's holy purpose.

The thesis of this book is simple: Charismatic churches in America today are laden down with tons of baggage that needs to be thrown overboard. If we would reject our misguided mysticism, our smug elitism and our hollow egotism, I believe our churches would be aflame with holy zeal. If we would renounce our bizarre infatuation with money and success, I believe, God would grant us true passion for the Savior. If we would stop mistreating the flock of God, He might give us many more sheep to tend. And, most importantly, if we would stop building our own human-centered kingdoms, He might afford us the honor of playing a part in building His.

I am not a theologian or pastor, so I do not offer in this book an exhaustive scriptural thesis on how we can secure spiritual renewal in this country. But I have made it my business as a journalist to observe the charismatic renewal movement—a movement of which I am part. This book is my feeble attempt to identify some of the reasons our fire is not burning brightly like the fire I witnessed in Cuba (a fire that is also blazing in many other parts of the world today).

Some two centuries ago the apostle Paul urged the Christians of Thessalonica to keep their fire white-hot.

"Do not quench the Spirit," he told them (1 Thessalonians 5:19, rsv). The Living Bible translation says, "Do not smother the Holy Spirit."

Yet since the first century men have frustrated the work of the Spirit with their own carnality. In this book, I point out six specific things that have smothered the Spirit in charismatic and Pentecostal churches in America: mysticism, elitism, separatism, authoritarianism, egotism and greed.

My simple prayer is that God would purge us of all these things, so that the Spirit can have His way. May God ignite a new fire in our midst and grant us a new Pentecost.

My Personal Pentecost

It happened to me in 1976. One hot Sunday morning in August, at a Southern Baptist church in suburban Atlanta, I had a profound encounter with Jesus Christ that set my life on a new course and redirected all my personal ambitions. It was not a spectacular moment by any means. The other eighteen-year-olds in that modest Sunday school room were probably daydreaming about their college plans or upcoming events on their social calendars. But June Leverette had my attention that day when she began her lesson from the Gospel of John.

"If any man is thirsty, let him come to Me and drink," she read in the tranquil drawl of a Georgia native.

I had probably heard that verse a million times. But somehow, read by this softspoken middle-aged woman that morning, it was amplified. I could hear behind her words the voice of the Lord calling me to Himself.

I was already a Christian. I had attended Southern Baptist churches since my childhood, made public professions of my faith several times and was a regular in the youth group. But when June began to read that passage from John 7 on this particular morning, a light went on inside me. I suddenly understood that Christianity was much, much more than Bible verses and church programs and Sunday services and senior high retreats.

Jesus Christ is not just a religious concept, I thought to myself. *He's real. He died on the cross for my sins and He rose from the dead. He's really in heaven, seated at the right hand of the Father. He sees me and knows me intimately.*

And I sensed that this Jesus Christ I had claimed to know for several years was calling me to know Him in a deeper way. I had never felt His call so strongly.

Yet I had no idea how to respond. And I was full of questions: *Is my Christian experience missing a vital ingredient? What else does Jesus have to offer me besides salvation? Is there more to the Christian life than just struggling to overcome temptation? Do the words of the Bible, which usually seem obtuse, contain a relevant personal message?*

"If any man is thirsty, let him come to Me and drink," June read again.

There was something uncanny about June Leverette. She talked about Jesus as if she knew Him—as if she had just had a conversation with Him in the car on her way to church. She seemed to exude joy and peace and love. She talked about prayer as if it were something adventurous and exciting. When she read the Bible, it seemed to come alive. I didn't know her well, but it was obvious she was the kind of person who could share her faith confidently with others. That was something I wished I could do, but the thought of witnessing to strangers mortified me.

"He who believes in me, as the Scripture said, 'From his innermost being shall flow rivers of living water,'"

June read. Then she proceeded to talk about the Holy Spirit.

The Holy Spirit gives us power to be witnesses, she explained. The Holy Spirit enlightens us to know God's will and helps us live our lives in a way that is pleasing to the Father. The Holy Spirit wants to fill us and channel the overflow of God's love and power to others. The Holy Spirit is our Teacher, our Guide, our Comforter.

It was obvious to me that June had encountered this Holy Spirit personally whom she was now defining.

Then another light went on inside me. In all my years of church activities, this was the first time I remembered hearing someone teach about the Person or work of the Holy Spirit. I am sure it was not the first time the third Person of the Trinity had been mentioned at the churches I had attended. But it was the first time I had ever listened. And when June Leverette began to describe how the Holy Spirit had become real to her in recent days, I hung on her words.

When the thirty-minute lesson was over, I knew I wanted what June had, whatever that was. I had no idea what a charismatic or Pentecostal was. I knew nothing about the *charismata*, or gifts of the Holy Spirit, and no one I knew in any Southern Baptist church had ever addressed the issue of speaking in tongues. Healing was not discussed either. Whenever we prayed for the sick during church services, we usually asked God to comfort the people on the hospital visitation list.

And so, in my naiveté, I asked June in a conversation at her house not long afterward to explain to me why no pastor of any church I had attended had ever discussed this so-called "baptism in the Holy Spirit" that she was advocating. She just smiled and told me, in her gracious Southern way, that anyone, whether a pastor or a teenager like me, could be filled with the

Holy Spirit's power. That settled it for me. I wanted to take the plunge.

A Vibrant New Faith

I had no fears when I asked the Lord to baptize me in the Holy Spirit. In the few weeks that I had spent studying some books June gave me about this so-called "second blessing," I had become aware that some Baptists disregarded the Pentecostal experience, and I had heard that a few of them believed speaking in tongues was from the devil. But as I studied the Scriptures, I could find no evidence that I should stop pursuing this spiritual experience. In fact, I took special direction from Jesus' words to His disciples:

> "Now suppose one of you fathers is asked by his son for a fish; he will not give him a snake instead of a fish, will he? Or if he is asked for an egg, he will not give him a scorpion, will he? If you then, being evil, know how to give good gifts to your children, how much more shall your heavenly Father give the Holy Spirit to those who ask Him?"
>
> Luke 11:11–13, NASB

I did not pursue the baptism of the Holy Spirit so that I could speak in tongues, prophesy or cast out demons. I simply wanted a fresh touch of God's power so that I could be more faithful in my walk with the Lord. I had struggled constantly as a teenager in my commitment to Christ and spent most of my time in spiritual defeat. I was weary of walking the fence, pretending to be a good Christian with my church friends while hiding my faith under a bushel at school. The revelation that the indwelling Holy Spirit could empower me to be a faithful witness was an appealing concept.

So, late in the evening on September 5, 1976, I sat down on a bench behind First Baptist Church in Avondale Estates, Georgia, and prayed for a personal miracle. I did not expect wind from heaven or a flame of fire to ignite over my head, but I wanted whatever version of Pentecost the Lord had reserved for me. I identified with the early disciples who tarried in the Upper Room for the promised Holy Spirit. Like them, I was familiar with the teachings of Jesus. I could explain the Gospel in simple terms. But I wanted the fire of the Spirit to ignite within me so I could turn my world upside-down, as Christ's followers had done in the book of Acts.

I knew this was a watershed moment.

"Lord, my life is Yours," I said. "Fill me with Your Holy Spirit."

I saw no visions, heard no claps of thunder or angels singing hallelujah in the eaves of the church behind me. The Holy Spirit did not descend in bodily form like a dove to rest on my head. I did not speak in tongues that evening. But as I sat motionless on that concrete slab, I felt the Lord's hand on me. I could sense that He was pleased. Although I had yet to learn to discern His voice in my day-to-day life, I sensed He was telling me that this baptism in the Holy Spirit was as much an act of total surrender as it was an empowering for ministry.

It was a long time before I stood to leave. As a muggy evening breeze meandered through the pine trees behind the church, I thought about the mighty, rushing wind that the early disciples had encountered in the second chapter of Acts. My experience had not been nearly so dramatic, but I knew my life would never be the same. I had encountered the Baptizer.

On Fire for Jesus

I did not now consider myself a charismatic or Pentecostal (though I did experience glossolalia, or speaking in tongues, the day after I was baptized in the Spirit). Nor did I know that I had become part of an extraordinary movement sweeping the world. All I knew was that my faith had come alive. I had a newfound hunger for God. I wanted to pray and study the Bible. I wanted fellowship with other sincere Christians. And I felt an unusual desire to impact my world for Jesus Christ.

Somehow I knew that the Holy Spirit's power would enable me to do just that.

My recommitment to Christ and experience of Pentecost came not a moment too soon. Three weeks after my unusual meeting with God behind First Baptist, I was on my way to college in the north Georgia mountains. Freshly strengthened by the infilling of the Holy Spirit, I found it easier to resist the temptations that await every high school graduate when he or she leaves home for the first time to explore life.

I began to fellowship immediately with a group of Christians on campus, many of whom had also recently experienced the baptism in the Holy Spirit. Before long a genuine revival movement was brewing at Berry College. Students staged prayer vigils for spiritual awakening on campus. Dozens of student-initiated Bible studies were taking place in the dorms on weeknights. Most importantly, young people were turning to Christ as a result of casual friendship evangelism.

In 1977 I had my first encounter with Maranatha Campus Ministries, at that time a relatively unknown ministry founded in Kentucky by Bob and Rose Weiner. Maranatha was the only distinctively charismatic student ministry on the scene. Pentecostal students were attracted to the group because the Weiners stressed that the baptism in the Holy Spirit was a prerequisite for living an overcoming Christian life. I was drawn simply by the fervor and devotion I saw in the lives of Maranatha's members. They were aflame with zeal for God. They were aggressive in evangelism while exhibiting a close bond of fellowship that I had not known existed.

It was obvious to me from my earliest involvement with Bob Weiner that Maranatha was a genuine revival movement. Young people came to Christ in droves in the early 1970s when Bob and Rose opened a small drug rehabilitation center in Paducah, Kentucky. More and more kids met the Lord as Maranatha outreaches were started on campuses like the University of Georgia in Athens and Mississippi State in Starkville. At the time I joined their ranks, Maranatha had chapters on twelve campuses in the South, and the first overseas Maranatha mission was about to be planted in Argentina.

In essence, Maranatha was an extension of the Jesus movement of the early 1970s. Bob and Rose had been involved in that unusual spiritual surge in southern California. Maranatha kids were adventurous, excited about fulfilling the Great Commission and very much in love with the Lord. Most of us were under the age of 25—there might have been a few gray hairs in the whole bunch—and we were as idealistic and gullible as young people can be.

Most of my Maranatha friends were making plans for full-time ministry, which we viewed as the highest goal attainable in life. Everything we did focused on reaching people for Jesus Christ. It was common for Maranatha students to spend their summers overseas on mission ventures.

I spent many nights conducting outreaches in the local campus union, showing evangelistic films like *Born Again* and *The Cross and the Switchblade*. I also joined

Maranatha students for weekend outreaches on other campuses, sometimes driving eight or ten hours to witness to students and counsel new believers.

The most logical step when I graduated from college was to take a ministry-related job with Maranatha.

What Began in the Spirit . . .

Although the ministry enjoyed favor from parents and charismatic leaders, Maranatha took plenty of criticism. Some of this resulted from our charismatic beliefs. But during the 1980s the most common grounds for concern usually involved reports of heavyhanded discipleship and authoritarian tendencies in our leadership. A report in *Christianity Today* in 1984 raised questions about many of Maranatha's practices. Some people began to suggest that Maranatha had cultlike tendencies, or even that the group might be a cult.

Bob Weiner did not help to allay those fears. His intense personality only reinforced outside observers' concerns that he wielded too much control over the organization and its members.

The cult accusations triggered self-examination on the part of some Maranatha pastors, most of whom had assumed their first pastoral positions in their early twenties. None of these men had any formal theological training. They followed orders obediently and treated their churches more or less like army regiments. Maranatha as a whole was administered like a military outfit, and we often prided ourselves in being "God's green berets." We sometimes mused that Maranatha was the contemporary equivalent of William Booth's Salvation Army.

Some of Maranatha's leaders began to realize they had indeed embraced some false teachings along the way, particularly the doctrines of submission and "shepherding" popularized in the 1970s and early '80s by the so-called "Fort Lauderdale Five"—charismatic Bible teachers Derek Prince, Bob Mumford, Charles Simpson, Ern Baxter and Don Basham. (We will look at the shepherding teaching in greater depth in chapter 10.) It became clear that these beliefs had caused much emotional damage among Maranatha's members.

Ministry leaders finally concluded that Bob Weiner had been abusing his authority as the so-called "apostle" of the Maranatha movement. Although the ministry had a board of appointed elders, Bob typically ruled with an iron hand and expected Maranatha pastors to govern their churches the same way.

A painful day of reckoning arrived in 1989. Weiner's authority was challenged by his own followers, resulting in explosive confrontations and a hasty decision to shut down the entire ministry. With no organizational structure remaining, each local pastor attempted to keep his own church afloat. Some of the men resigned their positions abruptly or pulled out of ministry work altogether. Others learned from Maranatha's mistakes and are still pastoring churches and conducting missionary work in several parts of the world.

A majority of the ministry's members scattered to the four winds, dispersing into independent charismatic churches as well as Episcopal, Presbyterian, Baptist and Pentecostal groups. Many became disillusioned with the charismatic renewal and the specific abuses they associated with their church experiences in Maranatha. Some became bitter. Others learned to appreciate the positive they had gleaned in Maranatha while rejecting authoritarianism and other negative influences.

As a survivor myself of this painful ordeal, I have spent plenty of time reflecting on the errors we made in

Maranatha. I have wondered how we came to allow something "begun by the Spirit" (quoting the apostle Paul in Galatians 3:3, NASB) to be "perfected by the flesh." I have questioned how we could have been so zealous for Jesus Christ while so prone to unhealthy spiritual influences.

I have drawn a few conclusions, all of which form the basis for this book. But my central thesis is simple: The charismatic renewal, particularly in the United States, needs desperately to return to the freshness of its beginnings. We also need to be purged of doctrinal error, some of which has tainted the movement since its inception. We need the Baptizer to send fresh fire to burn away all the trappings of charismatic religion.

I believe that the Pentecostal movement of the twentieth century and the charismatic renewal that began in the 1960s were sent from heaven. But God did not breathe renewal on the Church so that we could hang more religious structures and more intricate doctrinal requirements around the necks of our converts. No, the purpose of the charismatic renewal was to arouse a sleeping Church by sparking personal revival in the hearts of millions.

When I experienced the baptism in the Holy Spirit in 1976, my faith began to blaze brightly. Yet as the years progressed, particularly during the time I spent in Maranatha, what began in the Spirit became more and more regimented by manmade religious programs. It was hard to discern the leading of the Holy Spirit or experience the joy of the Lord when my faith was suffocating under the weight of legalism.

I do not fault Maranatha or any individual. Throughout Church history, revivals have always been smothered by religiosity. That is why much of the New Testament encourages us to keep the fires of faith burning brightly, and why the apostle Paul exhorted us not to

quench the Spirit. The New International Version trans-
lates his charge, "Do not put out the Spirit's fire" (1 Thessalonians 5:19).

I suspect that the flame at the heart of the Pente-
costal/charismatic movement today is flickering. The
Spirit has been quenched by sin in the Church—sin un-
confined to covetousness or sexual immorality. We cannot blame certain prominent television evangelists for
our own pitiful attempts to control the Holy Spirit's
agenda or regulate the people of God. Most of all, we
have been left dry and fruitless by our own complacency
and lack of desire for the presence of God's Spirit. We
need revival desperately.

In seven areas in particular I believe we Pentecostals
and charismatics have made key mistakes. And in this
book I would like to look at these areas chapter by chapter, first taking a closer look at the Pentecostal/charis-
matic movement in the twentieth century and concluding with some aspects of spiritual preparation I believe
we must make as we head into the storm already brewing around us—a storm that I believe is of God's making.

My prayer is that the Holy Spirit will visit us once
again to spark a new fire. We would be wise not to predict how a new move of God will emerge or what changes
it might bring. When God revisits His Church, it will
probably not be in the form of the charismatic movement
of the 1960s or '70s. It will be fresh, new. And it may
begin with people we neither accept nor consider particularly spiritual. Some of them may not speak in
tongues. They may not use the same religious jargon we
do. But if it is a genuine move of God, it will continue
the work of renewal in the Body of Christ and empower
God's people to take the Gospel to the world.

The Pentecostal Explosion of the Twentieth Century

Our world at the close of the twentieth century is in a state of upheaval. The turbulent changes occurring on the geopolitical and economic scene are so rapid and far-reaching that as soon as cartographers publish their maps, new borders are formed by a change in the Balkans or a breakaway republic somewhere in the Russian Federation. The very shape of our world is being redrawn, and the new maps are only outward indications of sweeping philosophical changes occurring on an international scale.

Post-Cold War societies are being transformed as their citizens slough off Marxist ideals and structures. A divided Germany, swiftly reunited, is now attempting to heal its wounds. The few remaining tyrannical governments, like the one in China, are losing control of dissidents and being pushed harder toward reform by Western democracies and human rights organizations. Developing nations like India are dismantling socialist policies and embracing the concept of a free market economy. The Muslim world, jolted by recent Western military intervention in the Persian Gulf, has been thrown into a tailspin.

For those with no faith in a transcendent God nor any concept of His providential hand in human history, the events of the late twentieth century have been little more than the machinations of men. The unraveling of the Soviet Union, fascinating as it was to the watching world, was due to economic factors, we are told, or perhaps to Mikhail Gorbachev's risky experiment in *glasnost*. But the question remains: Was the spiritual revival that began sweeping through the Soviet republics in the late 1980s a mere coincidence?

A genuine Christian view of history does not allow for coincidence or happenstance. It requires us to see God's unseen hand behind all the radical adjustments taking place in our world. It compels us to consider the sheer force of what I will sometimes refer to in this book as the wind of the Spirit—the unseen power of God at work in contemporary world events.

If Christ is truly preeminent (Colossians 1:18), if God has indeed "installed my King" (Psalm 2:6) over this earth, if He in fact does shatter nations like earthenware and exalt and put down rulers, then surely we can expect to see His hand at work in our modern world. Translate *rulers* as *presidents* and *premiers*. If God has exalted His Son Jesus Christ to the highest place and given Him a name that is above every name (Philippians 2:9), can we not assume that He has a divine plan for the nations of the world?

It would seem to any careful observer that almost every region of the world is presently undergoing a spiritual transformation. The secular media have at times acknowledged the growth of Christianity in places like Latin America and Eastern Europe, but American journalists are sometimes slow to acknowledge religious trends and how they relate to current events.

Barbara Reynolds of *USA Today* chastised her colleagues in 1990 for ignoring the spiritual factors involved in the collapse of Marxism in the Soviet Union and the Eastern bloc. Her comments came after conducting an interview with Romanian activist pastor Laszlo Tokes, who provided the catalyst for the uprising that toppled the Ceaucescu regime in 1989. "Why are people who identify God . . . as responsible for changing world events not taken seriously by the media?" wrote Reynolds. "In concluding that God isn't important, the press is trying to play God itself."[1]

David Aikman, an evangelical Christian and senior correspondent for *Time* magazine in Washington, D.C., has leveled a similar charge against his associates in the news industry. "The failure to observe at all, not to mention to analyze and explain, the rise of evangelical Christianity in the U.S. over a period of two decades must constitute one of the great modern blind spots of the American journalistic mind," Aikman wrote in 1987.[2] The rapid growth of Christian churches in the developing world is, in Aikman's words, "one of the great stories of the century," yet is rarely considered an important factor in news analysis.

The story of the century. That is how I would describe the quiet yet rapid growth of Christianity throughout the world in our lifetime. Consider these facts compiled from reports from various American mission agencies:

- 3,500 new churches worldwide were opening every week in 1990.
- The Church in China grows, some researchers estimate, by 28,000 new converts every day. In 1991 the Christian population in the People's Republic was estimated at more than 60 million.

- About 20,000 Africans convert to Christianity each day. Sub-Saharan Africa is currently believed to be about forty percent Christian. A comprehensive study of church growth in West Africa, conducted by Christian Reformed World Missions, revealed that congregations in countries like Togo and Ivory Coast during the 1980s were growing at a rate of more than eight percent a year.

- South Korea is about thirty percent Christian. At the beginning of this century, it had no Protestant churches and was thought to be unreachable. The largest church in the world today is located in Seoul.

- Some observers claim that Indonesia may by now be 25 percent Christian, but government leaders in the officially Islamic country will not print or confirm the statistic.

- There are about 12,000 remaining "unreached people groups" in the world, down from 17,000 in 1974. Thomas Wang, editor of *A.D. 2000 and Beyond* in Colorado Springs, Colorado, says missiologists project that the task of planting churches among these populations could be accomplished within seven years.

These and other global church growth statistics indicate that we are witnessing the initial signs of a massive international Christian movement.

The growth shows no signs of waning, either—which means that at some point this "story of the century" will be too big to avoid. Christian revivals are underway in the remotest areas of the world. God's Spirit is at work regardless of the political or religious climate, with or without participation from Western missionaries. As of 1991 there were over 37,000 non-Western missionaries on the field, and the number is growing (according to Argentine missions researcher Luis Bush) by fifteen percent per year.

Chinese believers are now reaching Tibetans; Navajos are being sent as missionaries to Laplanders; and Latin Americans are venturing to plant churches among Libyans and Turks. More than 8,900 missionaries from India ministered cross-culturally in 1988 alone, more than twice as many as in 1980, according to missions expert Larry Pate. In 1991, 33 percent of Youth With A Mission's 7,000 full-time staff members were from non-Western nations. By the year 2000, two-thirds of the ministry's workers are expected to be from developing countries.

Some analysts predict a surge of missionary activity in the Muslim world within a few more years, although it may not be carried out by ordinary methods. In some parts of the Middle East, spontaneous revivals have been ignited with little help from missionaries. George Otis, director of a Seattle-based mission strategy organization, reported in 1990 that "extraordinary" things are happening in the region that defy our traditional understanding of evangelism. Although few missionaries work in Muslim-dominated countries, he said, "God is clearly moving among truth-seeking Muslims" through so-called "power encounters": healings, dreams, visions or other supernatural occurrences that sometimes expedite conversions. Such events have been reported in Algeria, Tunisia, Morocco, Turkey, Saudi Arabia, Iran and Soviet Central Asia.[3]

Evangelical growth in Latin America is also accelerating swiftly. In 1900 South and Central America had only 70,000 evangelical believers. In 1990 the number had grown to an estimated 40 million, and researchers predict the figure will mushroom to 100 million in ten years. Multiplied by the effects of the charismatic renewal within the Roman Catholic Church in countries like Colombia and Brazil, a sweeping Christian movement seems poised to envelop the continent.

Nowhere is the "story of the century" playing out so dramatically as in the Russian republics. Intellectuals starved for spiritual reality after more than seventy years of official atheism are now pleading for Bibles and asking how to overhaul their ailing institutions with Christian ideas. Everywhere on Russian campuses, teachers are interested in religion. Western mission agencies have been placing Christian faculty members in places like the Department of Atheism at the University of Moscow and at the Higher Communist Party School—institutions that have undergone name changes and complete philosophical overhaul since Communist hardliners were removed from power in 1991. Churches have sprung up overnight in many regions of the former Soviet empire, some of them composed entirely of teenagers and pastored by young converts with little training.

How will this remarkable story develop over the next decade? Could this worldwide Christian awakening continue to flourish until it touches every nation? Could the same philosophical breakdown that occurred in the Kremlin in the late 1980s occur in the power centers of Islamic theology in Tehran and Cairo and Mecca? Could we see the impenetrable wall that still isolates the People's Republic of China from the free world come crashing down like the Iron Curtain? To some observers it seems inevitable.

One thing is certain: If the growth of the Church continues to accelerate exponentially, the world in a few more decades will be a different place.

The Winds of Change in the Church

As entire nations enter this tumultuous period of spiritual and philosophical transformation, the Christian Church (at least in the West) is also embarking on a stormy voyage. Intriguing trends have emerged during the last few years that signal drastic changes ahead for the Church as we know it. During this present season of international upheaval, God seems to be redrawing the map of His Church.

One trend that cannot be ignored in reporting the remarkable story of world evangelization—in fact, it plays a vital supporting role in the thesis of this book—is what some have called the Pentecostalization of the Church. It stands to reason that if present growth trends continue, Pentecostal or charismatic church groups will soon be in the majority when global Church growth figures are assessed. In the short span of time since the outbreak of modern Pentecostalism in 1901, Pentecostal and charismatic churches have in many countries become a dominant force.

When I refer in this book to Pentecostals, incidentally, I am describing Christian believers affiliated with churches and denominations tracing their origins to the Pentecostal movements of the early 1900s—Charles Parham's revival in Topeka, Kansas, in 1901 and William J. Seymour's Azusa Street revival in Los Angeles in 1906. Pentecostal denominations include the Assemblies of God, the Church of God (Cleveland, Tennessee) and the International Church of the Foursquare Gospel.

When I refer to charismatics, I am describing Christian believers who believe in the present-day operation of the gifts of the Holy Spirit but do not belong to traditional Pentecostal denominations. Many charismatics belong to independent churches, while others are affiliated with traditional evangelical and mainline denominations.

While most Pentecostals insist that speaking in tongues is a primary evidence of the baptism of the Holy Spirit in the life of the believer, charismatics do not place the same degree of importance on that spiritual gift. Because both Pentecostals and charismatics emphasize the need for the empowering of the Holy Spirit, and because both stress that the gifts of the Spirit as described in the New Testament are valid expressions of God's activity today, I sometimes use the terms *Pentecostal* and *charismatic* synonymously.

Fuller Theological Seminary professor C. Peter Wagner, a noted church growth specialist, now claims that the rise of the Pentecostal movement in this century has no parallel in all of history. Statistics indicate that denominational Pentecostals have surpassed all the Reformation Protestant groups in size. Due to explosive growth in the developing nations, Pentecostals and charismatics now constitute, after Roman Catholics, the second-largest identifiable family of Christians on earth.[4]

Some Roman Catholics worry about the trend because most Latin Americans joining the ranks of the *evangelicos* are former Catholics who severed their allegiance to Rome after encountering a living Christ. In some cities in Argentina, Protestant churches have grown 500 to 700 percent since the early 1980s, with a majority of this growth among Pentecostal groups. Two of the largest churches in South America, Jotabeche Pentecostal Methodist Church in Chile and Vision de Futuro Church in Argentina, would be considered by Americans classical Pentecostal congregations.

Pentecostal groups dominate similarly in Africa and Asia. According to missions researcher David Barrett, the only Christian groups there that are growing, with the exception of the Roman Catholic Church in Africa, are those in the Pentecostal/charismatic category (including those in the mainline denominations). Barrett wrote in a 1988 report, "The sheer magnitude and diversity of the numbers involved [in the renewal movement in the Holy Spirit] beggar the imagination." He added that Pentecostal groups were growing by nineteen million a year, with two-thirds of that growth due to conversions.[5]

The table below, an excerpt from *Status of Global Mission, 1993, in Context of 20th and 21st Centuries* and prepared by Dr. Barrett, outlays the number of adherents to the world's Christian denominations in 1993[6]:

GLOBAL CHRISTIANITY	mid-1993
Total Christians as % of world	33.5
Affiliated church members	1,726,420,000
Practicing Christians	1,259,691,000
Pentecostals/Charismatics	429,523,000
Great Commission Christians (active)	616,000,000
Average Christian martyrs per year	150,000

The following world statistics are excerpted from Dr. Barrett's *Global Expansion of the Renewal Across the 20th Century, A.D. 1900-2000:*[7]

	2000 (est.)
Total all pentecostal/ charismatic church members	562,526,000
Total as % of world's church-member Christians	28.60
Pentecostals/charismatics unaffiliated to churches or groups	56,800,000

	2000 (est.)
Total all professing pentecostals/ charismatics	619,326,000
Total as % of whole world's Christians	29.10

Although critics may quibble with some of these figures, the tables demonstrate the explosive growth among
Pentecostal and charismatic groups. Why are they growing so rapidly? Some armchair critics would argue that
most of those joining Pentecostal ranks in the developing world are poor, uneducated people who place little
importance on sound theology but are attracted by the
traditional Pentecostal emphasis on personal salvation,
healing and exuberant worship. Other observers say the
Pentecostal/charismatic style of faith offers a subjective
spirituality that many people, including believers from
traditional churches, lack.

Some Pentecostals and charismatics, on the other
hand, view the present worldwide growth of the movement as a vindication of their doctrines. Francis Mac-
Nutt, long a leader in the charismatic renewal, offered
this assessment: "I believe the spiritual message behind
these numbers is loud and clear: the power of the Spirit
is really needed to evangelize. If the non-Pentecostal
churches do not recognize the need for a Pentecostal empowering, their efforts to evangelize will languish."[8]

It is not fair to say that because non-Pentecostal evangelical churches do not emphasize the charismatic gifts,
they are ineffective in evangelism or reject the need for
the Holy Spirit. In fact, evangelicals have led the way
for two centuries in world evangelization and have
added immeasurably to our understanding of the Holy
Spirit's role. But it can safely be stated that Pentecostal
or charismatic groups are often marked by zeal and a

spiritual exuberance that tends to attract young people and new converts.

This is what has happened in Russia in recent days. When a reporter for *The New York Times* investigated the spiritual revival occurring in and around Moscow in the fall of 1991, he discovered that a growing number of Russians were joining charismatic churches rather than returning to the tradition-bound Russian Orthodox Church.

"The Orthodox churches are very beautiful, but now I think I want more than icons," one Soviet nurse, Zoya Chalova, told the journalist. "People laugh and are happy" in her charismatic church, she added. Chalova was seeking evidence of spiritual vitality, and she found it in the Christian joy and brotherly love exhibited in a charismatic congregation.

Many others like her are making the same choice. Where will this trend take us? How will the renewal movement and its leaders shape the Church in the next chapter of history? How will the growth of Pentecostal congregations in the developing world change the overall makeup of the Church? I have no doubt that the movement will continue to grow at an exponential rate.

At the same time, we face a challenge. If Pentecostals and charismatics intend to assume a more visible leadership role in the larger Body of Christ, we must first put our own house in order. Rather than pride ourselves on gaining a significant segment of followers, we must humble ourselves and admit the need for reformation in our own ranks.

As the wind of the Spirit blows through the Church in the decade of the 1990s, I pray that we charismatics and Pentecostals will catch the wind and be borne aloft, rather than become an obstacle to God's purposes. But that depends in part on how we respond to seven major problems that have indeed been obstacles since the outset of the charismatic renewal.

A New Wind
Is Blowing

Pentecostal and charismatic groups in the United States have become a major part of the spiritual landscape and have gained a large degree of acceptance in recent years from non-Pentecostals. The membership of the National Association of Evangelicals is now estimated to be 51 percent charismatic/Pentecostal, and its president elected in 1992, Don Argue, is a leader in the Assemblies of God.

We have come a long way since the days of tent revivals and backwoods camp meetings. Some of the largest churches in America are pastored by Christians who speak in tongues, prophesy and lay hands on the sick. Charismatics and Pentecostals are no longer considered the lunatic fringe of Christendom but are on the front lines—planting churches, establishing seminaries, evangelizing the inner cities, feeding the poor, taking the Gospel around the world.

Our churches are growing at a time when mainline Protestant churches are hemorrhaging. It is likely that within another decade the membership of the Assemblies of God could exceed that of the Episcopal Church or the Presbyterian Church (U.S.A.). In the U.S. during the 1980s, the International Church of the Foursquare Gospel, started in the 1920s by Pentecostal evangelist Aimee Semple McPherson, grew at a rate of 65 percent while it started thousands of churches overseas. By 1991, the Foursquare Church had 22,000 churches around the world, 11,000 of them in Brazil alone.

Data on the number of independent charismatic churches in America has been more difficult to collect, but there is ample evidence to suggest that these churches are growing at a rate faster than most. According to the International Megachurch Research Center in Bolivar, Missouri, the fastest-growing church in 1990 was World Changers Ministries, a black charismatic congregation in Atlanta. More recent reports indicate that the Church of God in Christ, a black Pentecostal group based in Memphis, Tennessee, is the fastest-growing denomination in the U.S.

According to missions researcher Patrick Johnstone, author of the 1993-updated book *Operation World* (Zondervan), independent charismatic congregations have become a force to be reckoned with. Statistics show that if all the independent charismatic churches in the U.S. were lumped into one church body, it would be listed as the fifth-largest denomination in the country. With some 2.5 million adherents, independent charismatics are dwarfed only by the Southern Baptist Convention (15 million), the United Methodist Church (8.8 million), and National Baptist Convention (8 million) and the Evangelical Lutheran Church in America (3.9 million).

There is also evidence, however, that independent charismatic churches in this country have reached a crossroads. This became especially obvious in 1992 when one of America's largest independent charismatic congregations, Chapel Hill Harvester Church in the Atlanta suburb of Decatur, suffered a sizable membership loss as a result of a much-publicized scandal involving several of its leaders. The church lost many of its 12,000 members after several former members told *The Atlanta Journal-Constitution* that they had been either sexually harassed or involved in illicit affairs with either the founder of the church, Bishop Earl Paulk, Jr., or two of the church's pastors. The women, along with many other former members, also told an Atlanta reporter that they considered the church leadership to be authoritarian and abusive.

Of the hundreds who left the church during and after the Chapel Hill scandal, some returned to the Baptist or Methodist churches they had attended before identifying with the charismatic renewal. Others opted to stop attending church altogether.

Situations similar to the crisis at Chapel Hill Harvester have caused many charismatic leaders to do some serious soul-searching. The inherent flaws in our movement are now becoming painfully obvious. Some of us are asking hard questions—about our doctrines, our methodology, our attitudes toward non-charismatics. Thankfully, a number of charismatic and Pentecostal leaders are addressing these concerns and navigating our movement cautiously into safer waters.

But as this tricky navigational exercise takes place, charismatic Christians continue to jump ship, returning to their denominational moorings or to other non-charismatic churches, often deeply wounded by doctrines or practices they have encountered. Many of these people are terribly disillusioned. Some charismatic Christians say they "burned out" because of incessant legalistic demands placed on them every week from the pulpit. Some have been abused by authoritarian church leadership. Others banked their futures (or even their life savings) on prophetic predictions that later proved inaccurate. Many were caught in the middle of bitter

church splits caused by power-hungry pastors accountable to no one.

What *is* happening to the charismatic renewal? What
happened to the fire that once blazed in our midst?

Relating to the Mainstream

The river of the Church is sometimes said to have
three streams—the sacramental stream (the liturgical
churches emphasizing the sacraments, particularly
Communion); the evangelical stream (the churches emphasizing preaching and the Word of God); and the
charismatic/Pentecostal stream (the churches emphasizing the gifts and power of the Holy Spirit). I have participated in each of these streams and am grateful for
their contributions to the overall life of the Church.

For anyone to denounce charismatics or Pentecostals
in general terms, or to deny that they represent one of
the streams of the Church, is unwise and irresponsible.
Many of the advances being made in world evangelization, as we saw in the last chapter, are occurring through
the pioneering efforts of the Assemblies of God, Youth
With A Mission, the Foursquare Gospel churches, the
Church of God (Cleveland, Tennessee) and hundreds of
other organizations and indigenous movements around
the world.

But change is inevitable and necessary. Those of us
involved in Pentecostalism or the charismatic renewal
are growing up. The apostle Paul's exhortation to the
Corinthians to "put away childish things" (1 Corinthians 13:11, KJV) is an appropriate directive for this hour.
It is time for serious reevaluation of the theology,
methodology and attitudes that pervade all churches
rooted in Pentecostalism.

Since it is human nature to revolt against maturity, my prediction is that the changes ahead for charismatic groups during the next decade will most likely be difficult, perhaps even convulsive. Some of the more independent charismatic congregations in America may not weather the storm unless serious changes are made in doctrine and practice.

God's intention, I believe, is to guide charismatics and Pentecostals into the mainstream of evangelical Christianity. It could even be that Pentecostal churches will *be* the mainstream in a few more years, thereby introducing sweeping changes into the entire Body of Christ. But this realignment may not transpire before charismatics themselves are refined and purified. The closer we move toward the evangelical mainstream, the harder it will be for us to swim with our excess baggage in tow. If we insist on bringing along our pet doctrines, our mysticism or our separatist pride, the sheer weight might drag us back into a peripheral backwater.

Sometimes I wonder if we charismatics missed the whole point of the movement we claim as our own. Everything we do and believe revolves around renewing the spiritual life of the Church, yet we feel threatened when other Christians experience the Holy Spirit in ways that differ from our own. Somehow we expect the Spirit to conform to our own doctrinal patterns. Looking back with the benefit of hindsight, some charismatic leaders today are realizing that we have spent too much time in doctrinal hairsplitting while neglecting the more important issues of the Christian faith. We have invented a charismatic version of Pharisaism, straining at gnats and swallowing camels.

It is my regretful contention that we charismatics have been guilty of furthering division in Christ's Body. In the charismatic heyday of the 1960s and '70s, we talked a lot about renewal in various denominations as a result of a new awareness of the Holy Spirit's work. Yet today a large segment of charismatic Christianity has become isolated and withdrawn behind its own organizational cover. We have built tabernacles around our experiences and erected higher and sturdier fortifications around our doctrinal distinctives when they are questioned by our evangelical brothers and sisters. As a result, many charismatic groups in this country have become ingrown and myopic. We have regarded the rest of the Body of Christ with disdain, presuming smugly that we have been set aside as the spiritual elite in the Kingdom.

Many times in the thousands of charismatic church services I have attended since I experienced the baptism in the Holy Spirit in 1976, I have heard prophecies I believe were from God relating to a coming world revival: "I shall move by My Spirit, says the Lord. . . . I will pour out My Spirit upon all nations. . . . The earth will be full of My glory. . . . You shall see nations stream into My kingdom in your lifetime." These words are being fulfilled today. The opening of the Eastern bloc nations and the former Soviet Union (as I suggested in the last chapter) prompted one of the most significant evangelistic opportunities of all time. The growth of Protestant churches in Latin America in the 1980s also set historical precedent. A revival movement of worldwide proportions is now underway.

Yet world revival is not taking place in the way many charismatics and Pentecostals expected. Some of us thought that when the Holy Spirit poured out His power, non-Christians would beat down the doors of our churches. That has not happened in every case. God has chosen to bless Pentecostal denominations, yes, but He is also pouring out His power on Southern Baptists, Lutherans, Mennonites and Presbyterians.

The largest church in the world in 1991 was Dr. David Yonggi Cho's Yoido Full Gospel Church in Seoul, Korea, yet one of the fastest growing churches in Asia is a congregation in Sumba, Indonesia, that claims Reformed roots. God's Spirit does not appear to be constrained by a list of doctrinal prerequisites.

Shifting Winds

The book of Acts begins and ends with intriguing references to wind. Most Christians, particularly charismatic and Pentecostal believers, are well acquainted with Luke's description of the wind mentioned in Acts 2:

> When the day of Pentecost came, they were all together in one place. Suddenly a sound like the blowing of a violent wind came from heaven and filled the whole house where they were sitting. They saw what seemed to be tongues of fire that separated and came to rest on each of them. All of them were filled with the Holy Spirit and began to speak in other tongues as the Spirit enabled them. . . .
> Then Peter stood up with the Eleven, raised his voice and addressed the crowd: "Fellow Jews and all of you who are in Jerusalem, let me explain this to you. . . . This is what was spoken by the prophet Joel: 'In the last days, God says, I will pour out my Spirit on all people. . . .'"
>
> Acts 2:1–4, 14, 16–17

The outpouring of the Holy Spirit in the first century, "like the blowing of a violent wind," provided the impetus for a movement that ultimately conquered the Roman world. The Egyptians, Medes, Cretans, Arabs and other foreign visitors to Jerusalem who witnessed the miracle of Pentecost had no reason to believe that the tiny band preaching on the street would soon shake the Empire to its foundations, but that is exactly what took place within three hundred years. Like leaven in a lump of dough, the message of Christ quickly permeated the known world and became the dominant force in all of history.

The Gospel that began as an insignificant mustard seed soon grew, as Jesus had predicted, to become the most massive tree in the garden. The sound of Pentecost's rushing wind, like an awesome typhoon, altered the moral and spiritual terrain of three continents.

The book of Acts closes with a different kind of wind. In chapters 27 and 28 we read the fascinating account of the apostle Paul's journey to Rome as a prisoner under the watchful eye of an imperial centurion. When the centurion declined to heed Paul's warning against changing winter ports, a "wind of hurricane force" (Acts 27:14) drove the Roman vessel from its planned destination and raged for fourteen days. The storm destroyed the ship and the whole crew nearly drowned, but God intervened miraculously, enabling His apostolic messenger ultimately to debark in Rome. There Paul preached the Gospel of Christ in the court of Caesar himself.

It is no coincidence that the book of Acts begins and ends with these references to wind. I believe it is the Holy Spirit's way of signifying to us that we cannot experience the wind of Acts 2 without encountering the raging storm as well. The same Jesus who baptizes in the Holy Spirit also baptizes in fire.

The violent east-northeast wind drove the Roman ship across the Adriatic Sea in the direction of Rome, while the wind of Pentecost flung the seeds of the Gospel to the four corners of the world within a few short years. The fire of the Holy Spirit provided the apostles with supernatural ability to carry out their passionate missionary endeavors. The early Church leaders had little to rely on in the way of human ability: They had no organization or corporate structure, no elaborate communications technology, no proven methods of evangelism or discipleship, no Bible, no seminary training. It was the Holy Spirit who enabled these unlearned men to turn the world upside-down.

Since the events of the book of Acts, Christians throughout history have hoped that a heavenly wind might blow in their day. Whenever the Church has experienced a lull in her growth or a dampening of her fervor, spiritual revivals and renewal movements have appeared on the scene, releasing anew the Holy Spirit's power to energize the Church for her worldwide mission. With each fresh revival movement, new ground has been claimed for the Kingdom of God.

The ebb and flow of the history of the Church has been marked by many such revivals down through the centuries. This was certainly the case when the modern Pentecostal movement began in the United States at the beginning of the twentieth century. Although tainted by doctrinal error and disfigured by human failure, the movement made a pivotal impact on the Church worldwide that is only beginning to be understood today.

The Pentecostal explosion has not been without its problems. Fast growth often produces mutation. It is difficult to deny that the Pentecostal/charismatic movement has produced good fruit: millions of people converted to Christ, churches planted, spiritual passion ignited. Yet in the short history of the movement, it has produced its share of wood, hay and stubble.

Those involved in Pentecostalism or the charismatic renewal have experienced the excitement of the wind of Acts 2. We have sensed the Spirit's anointing. Our churches have brought countless numbers of Christians into a deeper, more personal relationship with Christ.

Yet at the same time, doctrinal excesses, hyperspiritu-
ality, legalism and various unorthodox practices have
succeeded at times in discrediting what is valid.

That is why I believe we are about to be visited by another wind—a wind much like the one that battered the
Roman ship in Acts 27. It is time for those of us who believe in the gifts of the Holy Spirit for today to pass
through the storm and allow what is false to be swept
away. Many of the structures we have built over the
years could possibly be broken up underneath us in the
midst of the tempest, but our message will be refined in
the process. God cannot give permanence to the work of
our hands unless it has been tested. We must face into
the wind.

Rodney Lensch, a thoughtful charismatic leader from
New York, proposed in 1989 that God was bringing His
own version of Soviet-style *perestroika* into the Church:

> There is a sovereign "restructuring" occurring in the king-
> dom of God that doesn't make the evening news . . . but
> it is an undeniable reality just the same. Personally, in
> all my years of being a Christian, I have never known a
> time of such change, stress, and bewilderment within the
> Church.
>
> Everything seems up for grabs. The predictability and
> security of past traditions can no longer be taken for
> granted. It is as though we are walking in the midst of
> an ecclesiastical earthquake. Pastors are checking out
> of the ministry. Bishops are wringing their hands over
> all the problems in charismatic and non-charismatic
> churches alike. Sincere born-again believers are staying
> home on Sunday mornings and having church by them-
> selves because the confusion and frustration in so many
> local churches is more than they can bear.[1]

I believe, along with Lensch, that God is allowing this
seismic cataclysm to hit because we need to be shaken.

Our attitudes and approach to ministry must change. We need nothing less than spiritual reformation. How can such a reformation begin? I suggest we all start asking questions.

For some reason, most charismatics don't like to question the system. Despite the fact that Scripture enjoins us to "test the spirits" (1 John 4:1), we have a tendency to jump onto the newest theological bandwagon without even asking where it is headed. In the book of Acts, the Bereans were depicted as admirable believers because, after they heard the Gospel, they "examined the Scriptures every day to see if what Paul said was true" (Acts 17:11). In some charismatic circles today, such an attitude would be castigated as a lack of faith or even rebellion.

I am not suggesting that we grill our pastors, stage twentieth-century witch hunts or light up the night sky with the burning of heretics. But it is time for charismatics and Pentecostals to evaluate what we believe and why.

In his book *A Different Gospel*, D. R. McConnell suggests that charismatic believers have reached a crisis point:

> The charismatic renewal has reached a spiritual intersection in its history, and the decisions made by charismatic leadership in the next five years will, I believe, forever determine our place in the annals of church history. Nothing less than the doctrinal orthodoxy of our movement is at stake.[2]

McConnell does not claim to be a prophet, and his book set off a controversy of its own in 1988. But I believe he is accurate in identifying the crossroads at which the charismatic renewal now stands. The Church today still harbors false teaching, some that we invented and much that we inherited.

Reformed theologian R. C. Sproul has stated that he believes evangelical Christianity in America is on the verge of doctrinal reformation. I pray we charismatics are part of it. I would hate to see us close our doors, holding tightly to our pet doctrines while the rest of the Body of Christ experiences an invigorating theological housecleaning. Wouldn't it be monumental if, while some evangelical denominations purge themselves of liberalism and dead tradition, we charismatics could be delivered from doctrinal shallowness and malaise?

In the next chapter I will discuss a recent book, John MacArthur's *Charismatic Chaos,* that may be useful in helping to accomplish just that.

Bringing Order to Charismatic Chaos

In 1992 fundamentalist pastor and theologian John MacArthur released *Charismatic Chaos*, an updated version of his 1978 book with Zondervan, *The Charismatics*. In this unflattering but well-researched critique, he excoriates charismatic leaders for promoting false doctrines and blasts almost all the leading charismatic preachers. Not only does he blame the more extravagant television evangelists for promoting heresy; he accuses moderate and respected leaders like Jack Hayford, Larry Christenson and C. Peter Wagner of spreading doctrinal confusion in the Church.

Most charismatic believers dismissed MacArthur's book in 1992 with hardly a thought, viewing it as vitriolic and a tool of the devil to further separate the Body of Christ, charismatic from non-charismatic. And so it is. In his 300-page treatise MacArthur denounces all aspects of charismatic theology and experience. He lumps every charismatic in with the most blatant prosperity preacher and questions one of the most basic charismatic/Pentecostal beliefs by announcing that God no longer performs miracles.

The criticism *Charismatic Chaos* contains would have been easier for charismatics to hear if MacArthur had tempered his arguments with balance and charity. But by labeling all of us heretics and failing to acknowledge any positive contributions of the charismatic renewal, MacArthur lost the opportunity to gain a wide audience among charismatic ranks.

Too bad. Although MacArthur does not believe that the New Testament gift of prophecy still operates today, his book contains a timely prophetic message. We need to hear some of what he has to say and would benefit by looking past his unreasonable conclusions and taking some key points of his message to heart.

I am not suggesting for a minute that we compromise our beliefs or amend our doctrine according to the narrow theology of a man who discounts miracles and denies that God speaks to people today. But those opinions do not disqualify John MacArthur from the fellowship of the saints. He is respected by a segment of the Body of Christ and I believe he did us all a service by asking some hard questions about charismatic beliefs and practices. In fact, every Pentecostal or charismatic believer would grow stronger in his or her faith by reading *Charismatic Chaos* and grappling with the theological issues it raises.

While many of MacArthur's sweeping conclusions are flawed, some of his observations deserve our attention. In the balance of this chapter I discuss six of what I see as his most relevant criticisms.

1. Charismatics have been guilty of misinterpreting Scripture and encouraging a cavalier attitude toward the Word of God.

Because many charismatic ministers have received little or no formal training in biblical interpretation, MacArthur says they have adopted what he calls an "ad lib approach to Scripture." Too often, he writes, charismatics rely on subjective interpretations of a particular passage in the Bible rather than research it in context, linguistically and historically. Although we have a wealth of Bible study aids at our fingertips, charismatics often shun serious study and simply "ask the Lord for the interpretation."

As an example of this freewheeling approach, MacArthur tells how Pentecostal faith teacher Kenneth Hagin, Sr., once announced that Jesus appeared to him in a vision and told him that the apostle Paul wrote the book of Hebrews. Writes MacArthur:

> Scripture, of course, does not identify the author of Hebrews. Godly men who have studied the book carefully for internal evidence of its authorship generally agree that the issue cannot be settled with any biblical proof. That does not matter to Kenneth Hagin; he has his own private revelation on the matter.[1]

I am not going to brand Hagin a heretic based on this statement. I know too many committed Christians who are associated with Hagin's ministry to blacklist him, as MacArthur and some cult-watchers have done. But this kind of subjective Bible interpretation has no place in the Church today. It puts the believer into an awkward position, forcing him or her to choose one man's flippant "revelation" against centuries of theological research.

In my years of involvement in the charismatic renewal, I have witnessed countless examples of careless Bible exposition. One young pastor I knew tried to convince his congregation, by citing a few obscure passages in the Old Testament, that they should tithe thirty percent of their incomes to the church if they intended to please God. I heard another pastor suggest, in a reck-

less interpretation of 1 Corinthians 11:29, that if anyone was considering leaving that church, he or she would
be judged by God for partaking of the Lord's Supper.

Most of us laugh today at what goes on in the churches
of backwoods West Virginia, where snakehandling is the
central part of worship services. But this practice is the
direct result of misguided interpretation of a passage in
the New Testament that says believers in Christ will indeed "pick up snakes with their hands" (Mark 16:18).

I have never heard any charismatic or Pentecostal
preacher endorse snakehandling, but I have heard just
about everything else. In 1991 a popular TV preacher
gave an elaborate teaching from the Old Testament
about salt in the Bible and how it symbolized covenant
loyalty. He then mailed tiny packets of salt to everyone
on his mailing list and urged them to return the packets with their prayer requests. He promised he would
take the people's needs to a "holy altar of salt" where he
believed God would meet him in a special way to answer
prayers and dispense blessings.

Had he carried his shabby theological thinking any
further, he might have promised to slaughter a bull and
drain its blood at the brazen altar so that the people
could receive forgiveness of sins!

Much of what goes on in the name of charismatic Bible
interpretation today is actually an exploitation of the
Word of God. I recently sat in disbelief as a Christian
TV talk show host on a local station began peddling a
brand of "Christian" laxative drink made with hyssop—
which was described as a "biblical" remedy because it is
mentioned in the Psalms in connection with purifica-
tion. Never mind that hyssop in the Bible was not eaten
as a dietary supplement, but rather used to apply the
blood of sacrificed animals to lepers and others seeking
special atonement.

There is no question that we charismatics have been careless in our handling of the Word of truth. What MacArthur fails to point out, however, is that faulty hermeneutics are often the result of youthful zeal. Few charismatic pastors I know intend to skew the meaning of the Bible or mislead their parishioners. They may lack training or mentors, yet they often display noticeable passion for God and possess contagious enthusiasm for evangelism.

MacArthur also fails to note that the majority of charismatic/Pentecostal leaders are as offended by a flippant attitude toward Scripture as he is. The largest Pentecostal denomination in the United States, the Assemblies of God, emphasizes in its seminaries and Bible colleges the importance of sound biblical interpretation, as do the Church of God (Cleveland, Tennessee) and the International Church of the Foursquare Gospel.

Many independent charismatics associate formal theological training with liberalism and apostasy (not surprising, considering the orientation of most of today's seminaries) and have chosen to throw out the proverbial baby with the bath water. By rejecting such training, however, they estrange themselves from the wisdom gleaned over the centuries by the world's great preachers and theologians and leave themselves vulnerable to serious error. I hope today's young charismatic leaders will recognize their need for solid grounding in biblical interpretation.

2. Charismatics have emphasized spiritual "anointing" over godly character.

Too much importance, says MacArthur, is placed on spiritual gifts and not enough on godly living. Many charismatics would probably agree, given the rash of moral failures in recent years among prominent charismatic and Pentecostal leaders.

Even after evangelist Jimmy Swaggart was caught in California with a prostitute in 1991, his most faithful followers continued to gather at his church in Baton Rouge, Louisiana, to hear his weekly sermons. They seemed unconcerned by Swaggart's moral life. His sermons were still as "anointed" as ever. Apparently his spirituality was evaluated not by his lifestyle but by his ability to stir a crowd with forceful preaching.

MacArthur asks an insightful question: How does God measure true spirituality? Is it determined by how eloquently we speak, by how many supernatural visions and dreams we have per week, by how much time we spend praying in tongues? Or is true spirituality measured by our attitudes, by the purity of our thoughts, by how we treat our family members or co-workers?

I have attended charismatic churches where the entire service revolved around "the anointing." The music leader talked about "anointed" praise and worship, the preacher laid hands on the sick and proclaimed the presence of a "healing anointing" and people gathered at the altar to attain a "new level of anointing" for ministry. There was no exhortation to walk in holiness, no mention of repentance from sin. The Holy Spirit was treated like some kind of mystical force that could be summoned and activated at will.

Many charismatics reject this kind of sensationalism. Burned out on hype and pulpit showmanship, weary of learning 95 different ways to use spiritual gifts when they recognize more basic needs, these believers are in search of a deeper spirituality that emphasizes the fruit of the Spirit as much or more than the gifts. They are placing growing importance on the character of those who assume leadership roles in the Church.

MacArthur himself would have us banish spiritual gifts altogether, of course, since he does not believe they play a God-given role in the modern-day Church. A more balanced approach would be to underscore the words of the apostle Paul, who told the Corinthians that spiritual gifts are worthless unless they are employed in an attitude of love (1 Corinthians 13:1–3).

3. Charismatics must seriously examine the concept of extrabiblical revelation.

John MacArthur does not believe that the Holy Spirit communicates with people today except through the pages of the Bible. His position on this issue is extreme, since even non-charismatic evangelicals teach that God can speak to us through impressions, dreams, circumstances or other believers.

But he raises an important issue when he points out that many charismatics overemphasize subjective revelation. The words *God told me,* according to MacArthur, have become "the anthem of the charismatic movement."

I have heard this anthem sung many times since I was baptized in the Holy Spirit—everything from "God told me to put it on my credit card" to "God told me to divorce my wife." Probably one of the most extreme examples—one the entire world caught a glimpse of—was Oral Roberts' famous prophecy in 1987 that God would take his life if he did not raise $8 million for his City of Faith medical center. Roberts received the needed money to keep his hospital open for a short time but was forced to close it two years later. He subsequently told an interviewer that God had told him the mission of the City of Faith had been successful because it merged the concept of healing and medicine "for the entire world, for the church world and for all generations."

Other prominent charismatic leaders are quick to announce what God has told them, although their pronouncements often sound incongruous with sound biblical doctrine. I respect Oral Roberts for the valuable contributions he has made to the Body of Christ, particularly his launching of a university that has trained countless ministers of the Gospel. But these "revelations" should be called to evaluation.

Too often we use the words *God told me* to validate our own spirituality. I have seen certain charismatic leaders stop in the middle of a sermon, close their eyes for a moment, then announce that God just told them what a particular Bible passage meant. The congregation sat in awe of the leader's supposed supernatural insight.

I know of another charismatic leader who claimed to receive revelation from God on a regular basis. He taught that God was still revealing hidden truths about His plans for the end times, and that only the most diligent seekers would attain this knowledge. It later came to light that this man, along with other male members of his church staff, had been involved in sexual misconduct with women in his congregation. The women had been told that God approved of these sexual relationships because they indirectly promoted the Kingdom of God—by meeting the deepest needs of the ministers.

Joseph Smith, the founder of Mormonism, invented a similar doctrine also based on a purported revelation from God. Indeed, most of the core beliefs of all cults are rooted in teachings hailed as divinely inspired.

What we charismatics need is less gullibility and more discernment, learning to practice the simple truth of 1 John 4:1:

> Dear friends, do not believe every spirit, but test the spirits to see whether they are from God, because many false prophets have gone out into the world.

If we are careful to check every "word" or experience against the inerrant Word of God, we are better safeguarded against pitfalls.

Evangelical and mainline theologians generally agree that God has revealed Himself in two ways. First, they use the term *general revelation* to refer to creation, nature, natural laws—all of those manifestations of God that surround us—and all human beings, from birth to death. (See Romans 1:19–21.)

The second way in which God has revealed Himself is denoted *specific revelation,* and is limited to the written Word and what it tells us about the Living Word, Jesus (John 1).

Yes, God does speak to us in other ways, but what we hear is *not on a par with Scripture,* and we do well to use humility in checking our "words," impressions and experiences to see if they line up with scriptural principles, and in expressing to others what we believe God has said.

4. Charismatics should not use experience as a valid test for truth.

The modern charismatic renewal grew out of shared experience. During the 1960s and '70s, hundreds of thousands of Christians representing many different church backgrounds received the baptism in the Holy Spirit, spoke in tongues and were given other spiritual gifts. Many of these Christians, eager receivers like myself, validated their experience by searching the Scriptures.

As a Southern Baptist who recalled no teaching on the book of Acts from Sunday school, I remember the thrill of reading how the early disciples "began to speak in other tongues as the Spirit enabled them" (Acts 2:4). My experience was validated again when I read the description of how the Holy Spirit fell on the family of Cornelius in Acts 10:44–47:

> While Peter was still speaking these words, the Holy Spirit came on all who heard the message. The circum-

cised believers who had come with Peter were aston-
ished that the gift of the Holy Spirit had been poured
out even on the Gentiles. For they heard them speaking
in tongues and praising God. Then Peter said, "Can anyone keep these people from being baptized with water?
They have received the Holy Spirit just as we have."

Validating an experience against Scripture is one
thing. Validating doctrine against experience, apart
from Scripture, is something else again.

In John MacArthur's dispensational theology, of
course, there is no room for speaking in tongues or for
any modern-day expression of spiritual gifts, whether
they are recorded in the Bible or not. He believes, like
most fundamentalists, that the need for these gifts
passed away with the first-century apostles.

Pentecostals and charismatics, on the other hand, see
no basis in Scripture for such a position, especially since
the primary purpose of the infilling of the Holy Spirit
was the empowerment of the disciples to preach the
Gospel to the whole world (Acts 1:8). Since the task of
global evangelism is incomplete, charismatics argue that
believers today still need the anointing of the Spirit and
His gifts for evangelism and ministry.

But not all so-called "charismatic experiences" can be
validated in the Scriptures—a fact of particular concern
to MacArthur. It should be to us as well.

In *Charismatic Chaos*, he describes a vision related
by Roberts Lairdon, a popular California-based Bible
teacher who claims that Jesus Christ took him on a tour
of heaven when he was only eight years old. In *I Saw
Heaven*, a book published by Harrison House, Lairdon
describes what Jesus looks like: "He's 5 feet 11 to 6 feet
tall, and he's got sandy brown hair. It's not too long and
it's not too short. He's the perfect man."

Lairdon also says he had a playful water fight with Jesus in the River of Life. He says he saw in heaven a stadium full of people he claims were the "cloud of witnesses" mentioned in Hebrews 12:1. And he claims he toured a huge storage facility near the throne room of God filled with legs, arms, fingers and packages of eyes waiting to be claimed in prayer by people on earth who need them.

I cannot say that Roberts Lairdon did not have a vision of Jesus when he was a small boy. But it concerns me that some naïve charismatics who hear about this experience will automatically put it on a par with Scripture and use it to develop a unique extrabiblical Christology and theology. Their Jesus becomes a playful, sandy-haired man with medium-length hair; and the reason a crippled man continues to suffer is that he has not "claimed by faith" a new leg from the heavenly storage room.

The question every believer should ask, of course, is whether the Bible validates Lairdon's vision and his view of healing. In the description of the risen Christ in the apostle John's revelation, the Lord is described (perhaps in poetic terminology) as having hair "white like wool, as white as snow," eyes "like blazing fire" and feet "like bronze glowing in a furnace" (Revelation 1:14–15). Seeing the glorified Lord invoked in the beloved disciple (who at the Last Supper had leaned on the Lord's breast) awe and holy fear. John's vision included no mention of arenas or storage rooms full of body parts, although it does describe a "river of the water of life" flowing from the throne of God (Revelation 22:1), where it is possible theoretically to have a water fight.

All this is not to say that Roberts Lairdon did not have a spiritual dream about heaven or that he is not a brother in the Lord. I have no reason to doubt he is a committed, Bible-believing evangelist, and he certainly spreads lots of zeal for God in his energetic meetings. But we charismatics must take care that our experiences and teaching line up with the Word of God. Says MacArthur:

> Very few Christians are like the Bereans, who "received the word with great eagerness, examining the Scriptures daily, to see whether these things were so" (Acts 17:11). We must commit ourselves to searching the Scriptures, and let our experience of the living Word come from that, not from inner feelings, supernatural phenomena, or other potentially counterfeit or untrustworthy evidences. Then our experience will bring the greatest, purest joy and blessing imaginable—because it is rooted and grounded in divine truth.[2]

Every vision or dream or so-called revelation must be judged against Scripture, Scripture only. It is the sole touchstone for valid Christian preaching and teaching—indeed, for life.

5. Charismatics should reexamine their beliefs and attitudes regarding faith healing.

I cannot, like John MacArthur, dismiss the gift of healing. Charismatics and Pentecostals who consider themselves students of the Scriptures find no evidence in the New Testament that healing and miracles were given only to the early Church for a brief moment in time.

Jesus told His disciples (Mark 16:17) that signs and wonders would follow the preaching of the Gospel. (Although the last part of this chapter is not included in the two earliest, most reliable manuscripts, signs and wonders *did* follow the preaching of the Gospel.) Jesus also promised His followers (John 14:14) that He would answer their prayers. If His promise concerning miracles was intended only for the first century, then why should we not assume that only first-century Christians would have their prayers answered?

Missionaries from around the world today are reporting supernatural incidents of healing, from the jungles of Borneo to the urban centers of Latin America. In some cases these miracles have pointed large groups of people to Jesus Christ, just as signs and wonders did in the early Church.

In 1990, for example, two representatives of Every Home for Christ reported that many members of a South Pacific tribe were converted to Christ after their tribal leader died from an illness. The chieftain died, according to field reports, but was revived briefly as a result of prayer. During the time he was resuscitated, he told the villagers he had met Jesus Christ, and he instructed his people to serve the God of the missionaries.

The apparent purpose of that miracle was not to meet the physical need of the chieftain but, like the signs and wonders in the New Testament, to point people to faith in Jesus Christ.

Many charismatics have taken healing to an extreme. We have promoted the idea that God wants to heal all people instantly of all their infirmities—cancer, head-colds or hangnails. This has created embarrassment, hurt and misunderstanding, since all people who seek healing are obviously not cured. It becomes more distressing when certain ministers who claim a special "healing anointing" use smoke and mirrors to give the impression that people are healed when they are not.

John MacArthur has some strong words for those who claim to have powerful healing ministries:

> Think of how thrilling and rewarding it would be to have the gift of healing! Think of what it would be like to go into a hospital among the sick and dying and just walk up and down the hall touching people and healing them!

It would be wonderful to gather groups of people with the gift of healing and fly them into the great pockets of disease in the world. They could walk through the crowds, healing everyone of cancer, tuberculosis, AIDS, and countless other ailments.

Why is it that charismatic healers have not attempted that? Why not assemble all those who say they have gifts of healing and have them go out to minister where the worst needs are? They could start in the hospitals and sanitariums in their own area, and then move beyond to the four corners of the earth. Opportunities to heal the sick are unlimited. And if, as charismatics often claim, such miracles are signs and wonders designed to convince unbelievers, would that kind of ministry not accomplish the purpose best?

But strangely, the healers rarely if ever come out of their tents, their tabernacles, or their television studios. They always seem to exercise their gift only in a controlled environment, staged their way, run according to their own schedule. Why do we seldom hear of the gift of healing being used in hospital hallways? Why aren't more healers using their gift on the streets in India and Bangladesh? Why aren't they in the leper colonies and AIDS hospices where masses of people are racked by disease? It is not happening. Why? Because those who claim the gift of healing do not really have it.[3]

MacArthur reaches the wrong conclusion here, but I tend to agree with his point that much "healing" supposedly taking place in flashy American healing crusades is spurious. Actually, there *are* healing evangelists working today who are going into the hospitals and centers of disease. Carlos Annacondia, a dynamic lay preacher in Argentina, began his crusade ministry by praying for sick people in a hospital in Buenos Aires. When a young girl was healed after he laid hands on her, thousands of Argentineans began flocking to his evangelistic services.

It is certainly true that many people today are skeptical about healing claims, especially those made by TV evangelists. In 1992 *The Orlando Sentinel* investigated the healing claims of evangelist Benny Hinn, who prays for thousands of sick people in nationwide crusades. The reporter asked staff members at Hinn's Orlando Christian Center to provide a list of cases in which a doctor had verified that the patient had been cured supernaturally. The newspaper reported that the church could not provide one name. The next year a syndicated television program, "Inside Edition," employed some questionable tactics to try to prove that Hinn was fabricating the healings he claimed were taking place in his miracle services. The TV show said that people Hinn claimed had been healed were still sick when they left his services.

To his credit, Hinn took drastic measures to revise the way he reported healings on his own TV program, and he hired a team of doctors to interview those who came to the altar for prayer. And he told *Charisma* magazine in June 1993 that he would no longer allow people to say they had been healed until a doctor could verify that their medical condition had indeed improved.

John MacArthur is expressing a minority position when he says that God does not heal today. I know plenty of Baptists and Methodists who anticipate miraculous intervention whenever a health crisis erupts in their lives. The real issue at stake is whether God *always* heals, and how He uses healing to draw unbelievers to Himself.

The New Testament demonstrates that the gift of miracles is a strategic means to capture people's attention and point them Christward. When Jesus walked the earth, He operated in the miraculous realm—but He did not heal everyone He met. For every leper He cleansed, thousands remained in their mournful condition. He raised Lazarus from the dead, restored a dead boy to his mother and a girl to her parents, yet death surrounded Jesus every day and He did not clear out the funeral parlors of Galilee. Incidents of miraculous healing were meant to be signals, directing the people toward faith in God.

We must stop promoting the simplistic idea that God intends us to vanquish all sickness and death. If we believe that, then why don't we pray for fellow church members to be raised from the dead when they die? And what message do we offer the thousands of people who are not healed? What do we tell the brokenhearted mother who assumes that the reason her infant died at birth is her lack of faith? What do we tell the young man in a wheelchair who has been prayed for by every famous healing evangelist in America, yet still cannot move his legs? What do we tell the parents whose firstborn child is mentally retarded? Many of these people have been wounded emotionally by fellow Christians who insist that their miracle can be spoken into being by the exercise of more faith.

We need to develop a truly biblical view of miracles. Healings and other supernatural acts of God in the New Testament did not take place at the drop of a hat. Yes, sincere faith was involved in every instance. But the disciples did not casually throw the power of God around at their whim. They understood that signs and wonders followed the preaching of the Gospel, and that such miracles pointed unbelievers to faith in God. In Acts 9 all the people in the towns of Lydda and Sharon turned to the Lord after Aeneas the paralytic began to walk. Many people turned to Christ in Joppa after Dorcas was raised from the dead (Acts 9:42).

I would add that when the true gift of miracles is in operation, it will always result in a harvest of souls.

6. Charismatics should reevaluate the so-called prosperity gospel and its related teachings.

Perhaps the most grotesque offshoot of the charismatic renewal in the United States is the "prosperity gospel," the message that Christians can supernaturally activate material benefits whenever they please. This teaching— some charismatics have called it verbal voodoo—has brought reproach on the Church at large and cast all charismatics, understandably, under suspicion.

Thankfully, most charismatics have seen through the flimsy doctrinal framework of name-it-and-claim-it. And since 1987, when Jim Bakker's PTL empire fell like a house of cards, other prosperity preachers who taught a similar brand of health-and-wealth gospel have begun to lose their support base.

The Word-faith movement was popularized by Pentecostal Bible teacher Kenneth Hagin, whose teachings were passed along to a younger generation of faith teachers, including Kenneth Copeland, Charles Capps, Frederick Price, Jerry Savelle and Robert Tilton. Some of these ministers have modified their doctrines over the years, while others, like Tilton, have grown more extreme in their insistence that God intends for all people to be rich. (It should be noted that Kenneth Hagin, Sr., and his son Kenneth Hagin, Jr., have distanced themselves from many of the younger Word-faith preachers on the circuit today. The Hagins have stated that some Word-faith proponents have taken their teachings to an extreme.)

Tilton, a neatly groomed success preacher with a Texas drawl, hit hard times in November 1990 when ABC's "Prime Time Live" aired a report charging that he was misusing donor funds so he could live lavishly. Tilton fought hard to defend himself against the allegations, but the damage was done. Some Christian TV stations took him off the air, his support base dwindled and he was forced to lay off a large chunk of his staff. Because the Texas attorney general's office showed an interest in investigating Tilton for mail fraud, the evangelist portrayed himself as a victim of religious persecution and was able to keep many of his followers for a season.

Those who dismiss MacArthur's arguments against Word-faith teaching are likely to point to the good that has come from preachers like Hagin or Copeland. But that good does not mean we have to endorse every doctrine they promote, any more than we endorse everything taught by *any* teacher we respect.

To be sure, I do not believe we can discount the ministries of these men. They have led thousands of people to Christ and done much to assist in the building of the Kingdom of God around the world. Hagin's school, Rhema Bible Training Center in Tulsa, Oklahoma, has trained leaders who have planted churches in many parts of the world. For that we can be grateful. But we must also exercise the liberty to question the Word-faith message.

It is obvious that the result of the so-called faith message has not always been an increase in godly faith. The Word-faith movement has, in many cases, infected the Body of Christ with gross materialism. Rather than focus our attention on meeting the needs of people less fortunate than we are, or on reaching the unreached for Christ, the prosperity gospel has turned our concern inward, on how we can acquire more wealth, nicer cars or bigger houses.

A more balanced biblical understanding recognizes the pivotal role of faith in doing the works of God, and the spiritual power of speaking words of faith. But it also recognizes the sovereignty of God who "is in heaven; he does whatever pleases him" (Psalm 115:3).

I have not attempted to rebut many points in *Charismatic Chaos* with which I disagree. I have discussed, rather, the points that have validity for charismatics and Pentecostals in the Church today. It is a sign of maturity if we can receive criticism from a leader outside our own theological camp, rather than raise our defenses and characterize the critic as an instrument of Satan. If we are to weather the storm that I believe lies ahead, we must be willing to learn from many sources and throw overboard our excess baggage.

Each of the next seven chapters carries an important lesson from the short history of Pentecostals and charismatics that, if received and learned, will help us in the days ahead to reignite the power of renewal.

Building Walls Around the Anointing

Not long after I was baptized in the Holy Spirit, I discovered how the topic of spiritual gifts divides Christians. It was 1977, just months after I had renewed my commitment to the Lord and asked Him to fill me with His power. Full of youthful zeal and hungry to know more about Jesus Christ, I was glad to find a friend like Steve Youngblood.

Steve, a year ahead of me in school, was the most committed Christian I had ever met. He had been raised Lutheran but attended a Baptist church during his college years because he realized his own views were more conservatively evangelical than the Lutheran churches he had attended. He was an avid reader and his favorite books centered around the subject of spiritual revival. Before long he introduced me to the classic works of revivalists like R. A. Torrey, Rees Howells and Leonard Ravenhill.

Steve and I would talk late into the night about the possibilities of revival at our small-town college and in the Church at large. Sensing a call to full-time ministry, Steve was burdened by the seeming complacency of some of the Christian students who attended our weekly campus fellowship group. Our mutual concern eventually led us to begin praying together every night for spiritual awakening.

Besides being a fervent effort to improve the spiritual atmosphere on our campus, these nightly prayer meetings cemented a close friendship between Steve and me. We supported one another in every way and shared our deepest struggles and concerns. Although Steve was aware of my charismatic beliefs, the subject never became an issue when we were praying together, mostly because we were seeking something that transcended doctrinal and denominational boundaries.

Nor did I feel compelled to force my own experiences onto Steve. We shared a unique sense of respect and camaraderie that became a source of strength for both of us.

But after about a year, a subtle rift, rooted in our fundamental disagreement over the charismatic renewal, began to divide us. Steve was bothered by my involvement in a charismatic campus ministry, which he perceived as promoting division, while I felt the Lord was leading me to be part of the group.

I could not accept the fact, on the other hand, that God might not be leading Steve to join me. Rather than simply acknowledge that the Holy Spirit was taking us down divergent paths, I developed a smug, self-righteous attitude. Although I never articulated it, I believed that I had chosen the superior route. I was a "Spirit-filled" Christian, after all, and Steve did not claim that label.

The heart-to-heart fellowship Steve and I had shared cooled. Outwardly we were cordial, of course, but we stopped praying for revival. I got busier with my church activities and spent most of my time with charismatic believers. When Steve graduated from college, we lost touch with each other. I learned later that he had assumed the pastorate of a Baptist church in Georgia.

Years later I realized that what happened between Steve and me has occurred on a much larger scale in the Body of Christ all across the United States. The evangelical sector of the Church has been effectively divided into two camps—those who call themselves charismatics, who sometimes consider themselves a cut above other Christians spiritually, and those who have not experienced the gifts of the Holy Spirit (at least in a charismatic sense), who are often made to feel like second-class citizens in God's Kingdom.

We charismatics talk a lot about the "anointing" of the Spirit. In the Old Testament the act of anointing with oil symbolized endowment with divine power for a sacred duty (see 1 Samuel 10:1, 6; 16:13; Isaiah 61:1). In the New Testament, Jesus—whose very name, Christ, means "the anointed One"—reinforced the principle that God's work can be accomplished only with the anointing of His Spirit.

It is this obvious need for the anointing of the Spirit that prompts believers to seek the charismatic experience. Still, we must be wary that we do not see ourselves as superior because of our encounter with the Baptizer. Every time charismatics (recipients of the *charismata,* or gifts of the Holy Spirit, by very definition gifts of *grace*) see ourselves as special, we are in effect building walls around the anointing. We are hoarding the gift of God rather than sharing it.

Rethinking the Issue of Tongues

I hope I have already communicated that my main reason for seeking the baptism in the Holy Spirit in 1976 was not so that I could speak in tongues, prophesy or attain the gift of healing. I wanted more of God. I also wanted the boldness that the early disciples possessed, and I knew that boldness was a primary consequence of the infilling of the Spirit. I read and reread Acts 4:31—that after the disciples prayed together, "the place where they were meeting was shaken. And they were all filled with the Holy Spirit and spoke the word of God boldly."

I also read that the reason for the initial outpouring of the Holy Spirit on the Day of Pentecost was to grant *dunamis*, or power, to the early Church. The risen Christ had told His followers,

> "You will receive power when the Holy Spirit comes on you; and you will be my witnesses in Jerusalem, and in all Judea and Samaria, and to the ends of the earth."
>
> Acts 1:8

This is why I sought what I viewed as a second blessing of the Spirit: I wanted my life to affect those around me for Jesus Christ, and I knew I could not do that in my own power.

I did fully expect to experience the gifts of the Spirit after I prayed for an infilling, but when I did not receive the gift of tongues at the moment I prayed, I was not disappointed. I had not viewed the gifts as the goal of Spirit baptism and knew that I had been baptized in the Spirit. Yet I understood from reading the New Testament that the gift of tongues was available to all believers. I read in 1 Corinthians 14:4, for example, that praying in an unknown tongue is a means of spiritual edification. So I remained open to receiving the gift. Then, during my personal devotional time a day after asking for the baptism in the Spirit, I received a heavenly language.

The gift of glossolalia, or speaking in tongues, is, according to traditional Pentecostal theology (similar in many ways to charismatic theology), the evidence of Holy Spirit baptism. This doctrine is known as the "initial evidence" teaching. Many pastors in the Assemblies of God, the Church of God (Cleveland, Tennessee), the Pentecostal Holiness denomination and various charismatic groups purport that a person is not truly filled with the Holy Spirit until he or she has spoken in tongues. Some old-line Pentecostal groups used to teach that seekers of the Spirit's blessing needed to "tarry" for long hours at church altars waiting for the promised gift. Many people would wait for months or even years for that evidence that they had been filled with the Spirit.

Some Pentecostals today are softening this stance, partly because large percentages of their own congregations do not speak in tongues. A recent study of fast-growing denominations (funded by the Lilly Endowment) shows that only 25 percent of the members of some Pentecostal churches claim to have received that spiritual gift, although these people belong to groups teaching that Christians must speak in tongues in order to be considered Spirit-filled.

Jack Hayford, a veteran Pentecostal pastor and the most prominent voice in the International Church of the Foursquare Gospel, opened up a new debate on this issue recently in his own denomination. While he still strongly advocates the gift of tongues as available to all believers, he is calling for balance on the issue.

In March 1993 he told *Charisma* magazine that he does not demand tongues as proof of the baptism in the Spirit, but views glossolalia as "a divine and desirable provision to assist every believer in prayer and praise." He added, "I accept the testimony of people in differing traditions who claim they are baptized in the Holy Spirit, whether they've spoken in tongues or not. Still, as I minister within my own tradition, I urge people to expect to speak with tongues when they receive the baptism with the Holy Spirit."[1]

The initial evidence teaching has, in effect, forced division in the Church. It has separated the "haves" from the "have-nots." Many Pentecostals consider their non-Pentecostal brethren spiritually inferior, while some non-Pentecostals have adopted the dispensational view that speaking in tongues is a gift intended only for the early Church. Thus they believe that Pentecostals, by encouraging the practice of tongues-speaking, are promoting doctrinal error.

Is it possible that this colossal separation in the Church can be reconciled? I believe it can, but it will require some compromise on both sides.

"Do All Speak in Tongues?"

All the popular charismatic Bible teachers of the 1970s, like Dennis and Rita Bennett, Don Basham and Frances Hunter, furthered the doctrine of initial evidence. Most of those baptized with the Holy Spirit during the heyday of the charismatic renewal adopted the view that speaking in tongues is an essential ingredient in the Spirit-filled life. Many of the best-selling charismatic books of that period even offered practical steps to receiving a personal prayer language.

But in their popular book *The Holy Spirit and You*, the Bennetts offered an exhortation that deserves repeating:

> When a person receives the baptism with the Holy Spirit, it doesn't mean he's "arrived" spiritually. . . . Don't ever yield to the enemy's temptation to cause you to feel superior; pray for the fruit of humility; it is a good anti-

dote. The baptism with the Holy Spirit is just the beginning of a new dimension in your Christian life, and
it is still up to you whether you will grow or regress.[2]

I wish the Bennetts' words had been taken more to
heart. Too many of us charismatics became puffed up
with spiritual pride after our initial encounter with the
Baptizer. We elevated our own views and looked down
on those who disagreed with our interpretation of Scripture. Once I heard a prominent charismatic leader crit-
icize the teachings of family counselor James Dobson
because he wasn't "Spirit-filled." In this person's esti-
mation, even evangelist Billy Graham was spiritually
deficient—simply because he did not claim to speak in
tongues.

Perhaps it is time we charismatics reassess the meaning of the reminder of the apostle Paul in 1 Corinthians
12:30: "Do all speak in tongues?"

During the days I was seeking the baptism in the
Spirit, this passage perplexed me. By any modern definition Paul would be considered a Pentecostal. He declared in 1 Corinthians 14:18, "I thank God that I speak
in tongues more than all of you." But here he was asking a rhetorical question, pointing out that not everyone is endowed with the same spiritual gifts or equipped
for the same ministries.

He tells the believers at Corinth:

There are different kinds of gifts, but the same Spirit. . . .
Now to each one the manifestation of the Spirit is given
for the common good. To one there is given through the
Spirit the message of wisdom, to another the message
of knowledge by means of the same Spirit, to another
faith by the same Spirit, to another gifts of healing by
that one Spirit, to another miraculous powers, to another prophecy, to another the ability to distinguish be-

tween spirits, to another the ability to speak in different kinds of tongues, and to still another the interpretation of tongues. All these are the work of one and the same Spirit, and he gives them to each one, just as he determines.

1 Corinthians 12:4, 7–11

Developing this argument, he continues:

If the whole body were an eye, where would the sense of hearing be? If the whole body were an ear, where would the sense of smell be? But in fact God has arranged the parts in the body, every one of them, just as he wanted them to be. If they were all one part, where would the body be? As it is, there are many parts, but one body. The eye cannot say to the hand, "I don't need you!" And the head cannot say to the feet, "I don't need you!"

verses 17–21

Paul obviously believed that all followers of Christ could exercise the gift of tongues, or he would not have written, "I would like every one of you to speak in tongues" (1 Corinthians 14:5). But in no way does he imply that those who speak in tongues are spiritually superior to those who do not. And nowhere does he endorse the idea that only those who speak in tongues fall into a special "Spirit-filled" category.

It is time we charismatics and Pentecostals shake ourselves loose from the bondage of spiritual pride—the most insidious of all sins—and claim the rest of the Body of Christ as eyes and ears, equal members. If we simply accept the fact, as stated by Paul, that not all speak in tongues, then we can accept our Christian brothers and sisters as gifted in other (and equally valid) ways.

Non-Pentecostals likewise need to accept those who speak in tongues or exercise other spiritual gifts. Fundamentalist and evangelical leaders who believe that the miraculous power of the Holy Spirit was operative only during the dispensation of the early Church must not dismiss charismatics as ignorant and theologically misguided, an aberrant fringe group that has broken away from orthodoxy.

Perhaps as charismatic and Pentecostal churches continue to multiply, and as we rethink our dogmatism and doctrinal flaws, our fundamentalist brothers and sisters will reconsider the notion that the *charismata* have no place in today's Church, and more of our evangelical brothers and sisters will acknowledge that the Holy Spirit is indeed at work in our midst. Perhaps they will concede that we too have a legitimate role to play in the Body of Christ, and that our spiritual gifts and anointings can complement theirs. Perhaps they also will consider Paul's admonition in 1 Corinthians 14:39, "Do not forbid speaking in tongues." Perhaps one day both groups can say to one another, "We have need of you."

This kind of reconciliation is possible. In fact, it has already been proven successful. Several years ago leaders in InterVarsity Christian Fellowship realized that the charismatic issue had the potential of dividing their university campus chapters. Originally the ministry had been antagonistic to Pentecostalism, but discerning leaders recognized the problem early enough to avoid a major split.

Leaders of individual student groups began to encourage the adoption of what some called the "forbid not, require not" policy. Chapter leaders who did not consider themselves charismatic were urged not to forbid the practice of tongues or to teach against it, while leaders who were charismatic agreed not to teach that tongues is necessary or to require it as evidence of spirituality.

I hope that the Body of Christ will follow Inter-Varsity's lead and adopt a similar stance on this divisive issue.

What Does It Mean to Be "Spirit-Filled"?

A prominent California-based evangelist once told me a fascinating story about the early days of his work in Argentina. This man, originally from a Brethren background, was baptized in the Holy Spirit and went on to cultivate a dynamic church growth ministry among charismatic groups in that South American country.

Once, after he preached to a large crowd, an aging Brethren leader who had given his life to missions work in Argentina came over and spoke to him.

"This man was not a charismatic," the evangelist told me, "and he never would say he had the gift of prophecy. But he said things to me that day that were more prophetic than any charismatic prophet has ever said. He told me I would have a significant impact on Argentina, and his words were incredibly uplifting to me."

In this case, a man who did not claim to be "filled with the Holy Spirit" delivered a prophecy to a charismatic who, thankfully, was humble enough to receive it from him.

This man's story makes me wonder how much we charismatics have missed because we have closed our hearts toward our "unanointed" brethren. We have long claimed the "Spirit-filled" label as our own—understandably, since we have wrongly equated spirituality with spiritual gifts. In an effort to compete with charismatics, meanwhile, some non-charismatic groups have laid claim as well to the Spirit-filled label.

Campus Crusade for Christ, which in earlier years adopted an anti-charismatic stance, began promoting a tract some years back on how to be filled with the Holy Spirit. It made no mention of speaking in tongues, of course, but focused on acquiring power to be a witness. More recently, Southern Baptist pastor Charles Stanley released a book called *The Wonderful Spirit-Filled Life* (Thomas Nelson, 1992) in which he disputes charismatic doctrines and argues that every believer is baptized in the Holy Spirit at the moment of regeneration.

So who is right? Who is Spirit-filled and who isn't? I have visited dozens of "Spirit-filled" churches in the past fifteen years where, despite the exercise of charismatic gifts during church services, the Holy Spirit was little in evidence and not especially welcome, though their members would have denied this. Although most of them spoke in tongues, the Spirit was quenched by the pride and self-promotion exhibited in the pulpit.

In another "Spirit-filled" church I know, the married pastor was involved in several simultaneous illicit affairs with women in his congregation during the very years he was exercising his gift of "prophecy" in public meetings.

During evangelist Jimmy Swaggart's ordeal with sexual addictions, he spoke to his congregation in Baton Rouge about revelations and messages he had received from God, and many of his followers begged him for more "anointed" preaching. Just before he was caught for the second time with a prostitute, Swaggart released a new book on the subject of spiritual warfare.

Sadly, many American churches that claim to be Spirit-filled are filled instead with spirits of immorality, deception and fraud. No wonder so many disillusioned charismatics have returned to noncharismatic churches!

We charismatics must be willing to admit that the display of spiritual gifts does not make us Spirit-filled. This is not to denigrate the gifts, of course, or to downplay their importance in the life of the Church and in the life of every Christian. They are vital, and the infilling of the Holy Spirit enables a believer to tap into His power. But we must repudiate the notion that demonstrating the gifts of the Spirit somehow promotes us to a higher class in the Kingdom of God.

We will be filled with the Spirit if we seek His infilling constantly, if we stay yielded to Him and if we walk in obedience to His Word.

Priding Ourselves in the Anointing

Ron found Christ during the Jesus movement in the early 1970s. He had been raised in a Pentecostal preacher's home and had seen enough hypocrisy in his father's churches to drive him far from God. While he was in college in Tennessee, however, a young man who had been touched by the spiritual vitality of that era shared a simple Gospel message with him—and Ron promptly embraced the faith he had forsaken.

Married at 19, Ron and his bride spent four years preparing for the ministry at a Pentecostal Bible college in Missouri. Like many other energetic young preachers, Ron and Marie wanted to make a permanent mark on their generation. What they lacked in wisdom they would compensate for in enthusiasm. That was their plan, anyway. But their enthusiasm was squelched shortly after they entered the ministry.

The denomination Ron had joined moved too slowly for him. He felt stifled by the church bureaucracy, which did not always embrace his passion for winning the lost. Ron and Marie felt they were marching to the beat of a different drummer. Everywhere they looked they saw spiritual coldness. The churches in their denomination either lacked zeal (they felt) or were compromising the standards of holiness.

In this place of disillusionment, Ron met Wayman, a Pentecostal evangelist who had broken from the Foursquare Church to start an independent work. Both men shared so much in common that they became instant friends. Wayman told Ron it was futile to work within denominational structures because they become encumbered so easily with carnality and human control.

Before long Wayman and Ron began working together to build a network of charismatic churches that spread rapidly across the southwestern United States. The churches in the group, which came to be known by insiders as the Fellowship, were small but the commitment requirements stringent. With his intense personality and autocratic leadership style, Wayman kept enthusiasm at a fever pitch by challenging other leaders in the group to go out into the highways and byways and compel sinners to repent.

There is no doubt that the Fellowship made an impact on many communities during the 1980s, when Wayman's disciples were planting churches all over the U.S. and in many foreign countries. But there was a negative side to this movement. Although the group had been started as a reaction against denominational control, the Fellowship developed its own mutant form of sectarianism that became ten times worse than any control Ron had encountered in his original denomination.

The Fellowship became infected with a deadly poison— the poison of elitism. Spiritual pride harbored by the leaders of the movement soon contaminated everyone involved. Church members were subjected to a barrage of teachings bolstering the importance of the Fellowship in God's plan for the world. The theme of elitism was woven constantly into sermons. The line of thinking went something like this:

- Special servants of God are not accepted by the mainstream religious groups of the day and are usually persecuted by them.
- Only a small percentage of Christians are obedient enough to qualify for this elite company. All others fall into the category of *carnal Christians.*
- Those who are part of the special group should not associate with average Christians, lest their faith be weakened or their morals compromised.
- Those belonging to denominational churches must "come out" of those religious systems if they truly want to be used by God.

The leaders of the Fellowship during its heyday in the 1980s expected the movement to spread around the world. Yet by 1989 some of its top leaders had resigned.

Ron was one of the first to leave but he paid a high price for his disloyalty. Blacklisted by other leaders in the group, he was characterized as a rebel and a Judas who was "sowing discord among the brethren"—not because he had left the faith, but because he had severed his ties with Wayman and the Fellowship. Some people in the group expected God to pour out His wrath on anyone who dared turn his or her back on God's anointed green berets.

Ron experienced emotional anguish after breaking away from Wayman's control. Because he himself had preached an elitist gospel for many years, he wrestled with fears that he had failed or that God had abandoned him or that his ministry would never be successful apart from the group. It has taken years, in fact, for Ron to recover from the negative images that this insidious elitism etched on his mind and spirit.

Ron's story may sound extreme and the group he once identified with cultic. But his story is true and the sad fact is, elitism in one form or another is not uncommon in charismatic churches today, especially independent ones. It is not hard to understand why elitism is such a potential problem in our movement. The Pentecostal experience itself, after all, can be portrayed as elitist; overnight it can divide a church into the haves and the have-nots. After charismatic believers are introduced to the gifts of the Spirit, those with more carnal minds will easily begin competing with each other in an effort to prove who is the most "spiritual" or "anointed."

The root of elitism, of course, is nothing but spiritual pride—a demonic desire to steal the glory due only to God and give it to a group of people. (I have already confessed to my own spiritual pride that separated me from my college friend Steve—just another form of elitism.)

When this form of spiritual pride is nourished, it develops into the most grotesque deception of all—the idea that a group of people can actually dispense eternal salvation. Every aberrant cult that has ever sprung up throughout history has thrived on this lie.

Members of cults like the Jehovah's Witnesses or the followers of Sun Myung Moon believe they will go to heaven because they are part of a special group. Many charismatic believers today have flirted with this idea, too. We have allowed the deception of elitism to pollute the Gospel, which is at its core a message given to all people regardless of education, performance, race, sex, nationality or spirituality.

Keepers of Special Revelation

When Joseph Smith published the Book of Mormon in 1830, he claimed that God had revealed to him a new set of truths superseding orthodox Christianity. He claimed that Moroni, an angel sent by God, had brought him this new revelation and marked him as the apostle of a new gospel. Smith insisted that all the Christian churches of his day had become apostate and that God had hand-picked him to launch a new covenant and an elite new church to bring salvation to the world.

So the Mormon religion was born. Smith, a man of questionable credentials whose lifestyle was tainted by immorality, became the prophet of a cultic movement that now claims nearly seven million adherents worldwide.

Smith's Church of Jesus Christ of Latter-day Saints is a movement rooted in elitist spirituality. Its founding doctrines stated that God replaced Christianity with Mormon doctrines like polygamy and baptism for the dead. Smith's followers built their religion around an elitist subculture: They rejected interaction with nonbelievers and promoted the idea that only faithful Mormons who adhere to certain laws of moral conduct can obtain salvation. Getting to heaven is far more complicated than a simple act of faith in the Savior. Mormons must (among other things) evangelize, strive to do good works, abstain from alcohol, bear children and participate in occult temple ceremonies in which they are entrusted with secret spiritual knowledge.

Most evangelical Christians need no convincing that Mormonism contradicts the essence of the Gospel. But why is it so hard for us to detect a similar elite spirit when it is evident in one of our own churches? Unlike the Mormons, charismatic groups are not promoting heresies that distort the character and mission of Christ. But many of us have flirted with the same demonic doctrines that enticed Joseph Smith.

The Latter Rain movement of the 1950s is known as a pivotal time in the history of Pentecostal churches in the U.S. Pentecostal leaders had begun to seek and promote "new truths." As churches embraced a deeper understanding of some aspects of the faith, they encountered resistance from less progressive denominational officials. This created divisions and splinter groups.

A verse from Isaiah burned into the hearts of the leaders of the Latter Rain era: "See, I am doing a new thing! Now it springs up; do you not perceive it?" (Isaiah 43:19). Members of Latter Rain churches began searching for new revelation, for the so-called "deeper truths." All they saw in their own churches was spiritual complacency. They longed for God to do a new thing in the Body of Christ.

This was a noble desire, but history tells us that in some instances it led to deception. The Latter Rain movement produced some healthy fruit in the Church and launched some significant ministries, but it also was rife with elitist doctrines. A major by-product of the movement was an endless list of teachings, usually derived from the Old Testament, promoting the idea that God has a special "end-time church" that will overshadow all previous generations of believers.

During this era many charismatic and Pentecostal groups retreated into their own subculture. They developed attitudes of self-importance. Many believers groped to identify themselves with the group that had been specially approved by God to usher in His Kingdom. Latter Rain teachings included these:

- Jesus' symbolic act of saving the best wine for last at the wedding of Cana was a prophetic sign that He would save the "best" spiritual anointing and revelation for the last generation of Christians.
- Benjamin, the younger brother of Joseph, was a spiritual type or foreshadowing of the elite "end-

time" church, which will be considered by God "a favored son."

- Jonathan's decision to remain with his father Saul rather than defect to David's army was a warning to those who chose to stay loyal to denominational churches.

The basic message promoted by these Latter Rain groups was simple: God has a special generation and we are it. Thus, even the praise and worship choruses that emerged from these groups focused more on the glory of the group than the glory of God. This has continued today. In many charismatic and Pentecostal churches, militant songs about the "army of God" and the "chosen generation" have in some cases served to strengthen this unhealthy focus.

Elitist teachings planted the seed of spiritual pride in those not on guard against deception. Certain churches began to describe themselves as "prophetic" groups—those with a corner on whatever truth they felt God was revealing at that hour. Many Christians began to hop from one church to another searching for the group with a monopoly on special revelation.

Return of the Apostles

A major tenet of Latter Rain teaching was the idea that God had never abolished the office of the apostle. Latter Rain churches emphasized the importance of Ephesians 4:11, in which the "fivefold ministry"—apostle, prophet, evangelist, pastor and teacher—is delineated.

Opinions among Bible scholars on this subject differ. Many of them, including some Pentecostals and charismatics, reject the concept that apostles still function today. The office of apostle, they teach, was reserved for the men who walked with Jesus Christ, witnessed His resurrection or (as in the case of Paul) encountered Him by special revelation. They esteem the apostles above others because they wrote the New Testament and pioneered the Church in the first century. Others insist that apostles are simply missionaries or church planters who initiate the work of the ministry in a given location.

In any case, the idea was circulated during the Latter Rain movement that an all-conquering, overcoming end-time Church would not become visible until an elite band of end-time apostles emerged to lead her.

This idea, of course, set the stage for failure. Like any movement based on one person's personality, it foundered. The so-called prophets and apostles of the Latter Rain movement proved to be as human as every other generation of Christian leaders.

But the deceptions of the Latter Rain movement did not die out in the 1950s. Most of the concepts taught in Latter Rain churches have resurfaced in many contemporary charismatic congregations. Why? The deception of elitism is alive in our congregations, still driving believers to search from church to church until they can identify that special group ordained by God for a higher purpose.

God Is No Respecter of Persons

Pride and the lust for acceptance are at the root of the venom we call elitism. Those who struggle to find their acceptance and identity in Christ fall easily into the trap of seeking acceptance in the "special group." Among unbelievers this is manifested in an identification with nationalist groups and elite clubs. In the Church it is evident when Christians place more stock in the importance of identifying with a particular group—even a very spiritual prayer group, say—than in freely sharing the love of God.

Elitism, whether among Baptists, Episcopalians or Pentecostals, is an affront to God. Elitism says, "It's not enough to know Christ. In order to be truly approved by God, you must enlist in His special army. You must commit yourself to my particular church or fellowship and be found among the ranks of the anointed." This heresy is the cornerstone of every pseudo-Christian cult that has ever littered the Kingdom.

The promise of eternal life through unmerited grace and salvation by faith in Christ alone is an invitation extended to individuals, not groups. God does not determine my fitness for heaven on the basis of what church I attend, nor does He evaluate my spirituality on the basis of what group I associate with or what apostle or prophet I follow. In fact, if I base my walk with God on my identity with any group or individual, I am guilty of *idolatry*—trusting in something other than God to secure my spiritual success.

Only God knows hearts. He knows the evil that can lurk in the heart of a preacher who commands the attention and awe of millions of television viewers. He knows the purity and simple devotion in the heart of a newly converted prison inmate. He sees beyond titles and college degrees and wealth. He looks past class status and religious affiliations and racial stigmas.

Some Christians today believe they have been set apart by God simply because they are charismatic or because they listen to Pastor Big Shot's anointed preaching every Sunday. Many of us will be shocked when we stand before God on the Day of Judgment and learn that He is lavishing His favor on the quiet Sunday school teacher at First Methodist who stayed humble before

God, kept her faith in Christ alone and devoted her life to imparting the Gospel to schoolchildren.

The spiritual revival that most charismatics and Pentecostals long for would be hastened if we stopped preaching an elitist, human-centered gospel and returned to the essence of Pentecost—a bold, Spirit-anointed proclamation of the Word of God to all people.

Had the 120 believers who gathered in the Upper Room on the Day of Pentecost been elitist, I doubt they would have scattered to spread the Good News. They would have created the Upper Room Fellowship, congratulated themselves on spending so much time in prayer and spent the next few years prophesying about how God would use them to win the world.

Elitism is, at its core, a byproduct of humanism. As the elevation of human strength and human institutions, elitism is doomed to failure. If we do not root it out of our churches, it will destroy us. Instead of directing people to applaud and admire their spiritual leaders, denominations and affiliations, we should return to the simple truth set forth in Romans 3:10–12:

> "There is no one righteous, not even one; there is no one who understands, no one who seeks God. All have turned away, they have together become worthless; there is no one who does good, not even one."

Nowhere does Scripture foretell a special breed of Christians who will one day surpass all others in their spirituality, and the sooner we banish this perverse doctrine from our midst the better. The Bible is clear. All men and women fall into one category: unrighteous. The Church is not compartmentalized by rank and we have no business dividing it. God has ordained one glorious Church, the unified Body of Christ made up of countless individuals who have appropriated by faith the atonement provided by Jesus Christ, the Savior.

Elitism in charismatic churches has been a major obstacle to denominational unity, and more and more leaders within our movement are recognizing that we cannot let the poison of spiritual pride isolate us from the rest of the Church.

Exploiting the Anointing

$\mathbb{C}$ hristians sympathetic to the charismatic renewal believe that one of the primary purposes of the Pentecostal outpouring at the beginning of this century was to bring about in the Church a restoration of the gifts of the Holy Spirit. Although many evangelical denominations still subscribe to the belief that the spiritual gifts listed in 1 Corinthians 12 are no longer in operation,[1] a growing percentage of believers today have come to accept prophecy, healing, speaking in tongues and other *charismata* as valid expressions of the Spirit's work.

Indeed, this belief in the gifts of the Spirit is central to understanding the dynamic growth of the charismatic movement and its popular appeal. The typical charismatic or Pentecostal believer trusts in a God who is actively at work in the world today. Charismatic Christians maintain that Jesus Christ still speaks, still heals the sick, still delivers the oppressed from demonic torment. The Christ who walked the streets of Galilee two thousand years ago "is the same yesterday and today and forever" (Hebrews 13:8) and He expresses His life through His indwelling Spirit in the Church.

Supernatural healings, divine guidance and miraculous answers to prayer are viewed as clear evidence of Christ's modern-day ministry on earth.

Yet at the same time that the gifts of the Spirit have been reclaimed by Christians worldwide, they also have been misused and abused, either intentionally by charlatans or unintentionally by misguided believers. The giftings of God, intended to strengthen the faith of individual Christians and equip the Church for the task of world evangelization, have been prostituted for personal gain and cheapened in the eyes of the Church and the world. In some cases, the abuse of spiritual gifts has so repulsed believers that it has triggered a backlash against the very renewal of the Church.

The essence of the charismatic experience requires openness to God's supernatural workings. Yet such openness poses potential problems and requires believers to exercise careful discernment. While the apostle Paul exhorted his followers to exercise spiritual gifts (he himself claimed to have seen visions and experienced other supernatural phenomena), he also cautioned the early Church to test the validity of prophecies, visions and angelic visitations (see 1 Corinthians 12:1–3; 14:6–40; Galatians 1:6–9).

We know from Paul's admonitions to the Corinthians, for example, that the believers there were misusing the gift of tongues, promoting heretical doctrines in their "prophecies" and constantly interrupting church meetings to convey unorthodox "revelations."

Paul warned the Colossians that they were in danger of being defrauded by people claiming to have exclusive access to divine revelation or special spiritual power. He told them, "Do not let anyone who delights in false humility and the worship of angels disqualify you for the prize. Such a person goes into great detail about what he has seen, and his unspiritual mind puffs him up with idle notions" (Colossians 2:18). The church in Colosse apparently had a problem with self-proclaimed mystics who felt they were called by God to impose their perverse views on the congregation. Churches are always debilitated, sometimes irreparably, when this kind of misguided mysticism continues unchecked.

The confusion that characterized the churches at Corinth and Colosse resembles the current state of affairs in the indigenous underground house churches in the People's Republic of China. Although the Church in that country is growing explosively, the lack of Bibles and trained leaders has produced a movement fraught with heresy, doctrinal division and bizarre practices. In 1992 News Network International reported that one fast-growing house church movement in China teaches that only those believers who have heard the voice of God audibly can be assured of salvation. Another group teaches that the Holy Spirit can be invoked when believers remove their clothes and dance together.[2]

These may seem like outlandish examples, but Pentecostals in the United States have promoted equally ridiculous doctrines by way of visions, dreams and "words from the Lord." Entire denominations have split over foolish directives given by hyperspiritual "prophets" who claim an inside connection to the Holy Spirit. Sadly, many of the highly acclaimed Pentecostal pioneers themselves veered away from biblical faith and became mired in deception.

Mysticism Run Amok: The Case of the Kansas City Prophets

Because the Pentecostal experience has been part of American church life for almost a century, and Pentecostal groups have had time to mature, the rampant, chaotic mysticism characterizing the Chinese house church movement is not a norm in the United States. Older Pentecostal churches have learned from past mistakes. Theology and methodology have been hammered out over time. And charismatic groups today (though younger than Pentecostals) tend to place greater priority on Bible training. Also, church members have become more adept at discerning between the genuine anointing of the Holy Spirit and fleshly or outright fraudulent attempts to duplicate that anointing.

Yet because charismatic believers fervently desire to witness a restoration of the Holy Spirit's power in the Church, they may be open to the supernatural in a naïve way, which often invites deception. As a result, charismatics have been duped by men and women who claim special spiritual powers.

Such was the case in the mid-1980s when Bob Jones arrived on the scene. A jovial, heavyset man from the hills of Arkansas, Jones had a penchant for delivering unusual prophecies during worship services. He had several run-ins with charismatic pastors until Mike Bickle, the zealous young leader of Kansas City Fellowship in Grandview, Missouri, took Jones under his wing and provided him with a platform for ministry.

For several years Jones was the darling of Kansas City Fellowship's growing church network, and his prophecies and visions were heralded as important foundations for Bickle's movement. Thousands of cassette tapes bearing Jones' peculiar testimonies and teachings began circulating among charismatic churches throughout the United States and in many foreign countries. Some of those who believed that Jones was one of God's special "end-time prophets" actually quit their jobs and moved to Kansas City to be closer to the "anointing" they believed emanated from that church.

Jones was touted by Bickle and other leaders outside Kansas City Fellowship as a New Testament "seer," a prophet with extraordinary insights into spiritual mysteries. In numerous church gatherings and conferences around the country, congregations were told that Jones received between five and ten "technicolor visions" from God each night. He was said to take frequent out-of-body excursions to heaven and hell, could see and converse with demon spirits and had numerous encounters with angels, one reportedly wearing red sunglasses. Jones once told church members that God might speak to them in their dreams by using the face and voice of Bob Jones.

What Jones offered his followers was a steady diet of visions, dreams and prophecies all reinforcing his image as a divinely inspired revelator on the level with Ezekiel or Jeremiah. He told members of Kansas City Fellowship that God visited him each year on the Day of Atonement and unveiled vital information about the events of the coming year.

Not only did the church eagerly await these annual revelations, they accepted an accompanying teaching he called "the Shepherd's rod." All believers on the Day of Atonement, according to Jones, are subjected to a sort of annual inspection in which God searches for hidden sin. Declaring that he had "all the Scriptures" to back up this doctrine but citing none of them, Jones told an audience in 1989 that when believers go under the Shepherd's rod, "He just turns you upside-down and He looks at every place on your body."[3]

Bob Jones' continuous prophecies and revelations ranged from the bizarre to the absurd. But because Bickle and other leaders at Kansas City Fellowship applauded him as a special messenger from God, members of that church as well as charismatic Christians all over the country were abuzz with excitement about what they called a "spirit of revival" brooding over Kansas City.

Few questioned Jones' validity, not even when his bold prophetic statements proved untrue.

Jones was particularly prone to predicting judgments of all kinds. He started this early in his career, before his involvement with Mike Bickle. While attending a charismatic Baptist church in the 1970s, he was known to interrupt services to prophesy about forthcoming earthquakes and other cataclysmic events. In 1989 he declared that God had told him one thousand religious leaders would die within one year because they would not pass the Shepherd's rod test.

Most of Jones' prophetic statements were so subjective they could not be verified. He told the congregation, for instance, that their movement was destined to become one of the greatest centers of spiritual revival in the world, and that 35 of the "apostles" who would emerge from Kansas City Fellowship would rival the apostle Paul.[4] This information was confirmed to him, Jones also said, during a visit with the two angels present at the resurrection of Christ. (Jones claimed frequent visits with angels, or at least to have overheard their conversations with one another. He often claimed to see angelic beings floating over the congregation or near the podium at Kansas City Fellowship.)

Once, after a member of the church had a miscarriage, Jones reportedly told her that for every drop of blood the baby lost, a soul would be saved in Wichita.[5] He told another woman that he knew she had received a special anointing because her hand turned purple after he squeezed it. Jones claimed to have the ability to discern spiritual strengths and weaknesses in others, albeit through an unorthodox method. He told members of Kansas City Fellowship that his body acted as a kind of spiritual Geiger counter, sending him messages via various sensations. If a person was involved in rebellion, a bitter taste in Jones' mouth was the appropriate signal.

He could also "smell" homosexuality, "feel" witchcraft and "taste" the presence of the Lord in a person. This means of spiritual communication was readily accepted by the rest of the congregation.

It is no wonder someone in the Kansas City area finally blew the whistle on Bob Jones and demanded that leaders in the Body of Christ examine his claims. Ernest Gruen, at that time pastor of Full Faith Church of Love in Shawnee, Kansas, publicly charged Kansas City Fellowship with heresy in 1990 and started a correction process. Jones was moved quietly to a more subordinate role on the church staff. About a year later, after the church had become affiliated with John Wimber's Vineyard network of churches, Jones admitted to a moral failure and was removed from his leadership position.[6]

Later Mike Bickle stated publicly that he had promoted Jones improperly. He admitted that his church's emphasis on prophecy and mystical experiences had been unhealthy and destructive.

In a 1993 interview published in *Charisma,* Bickle said he made four specific mistakes during his days as founding pastor of Kansas City Fellowship: (1) promoting elitism, which he described as "repulsive"; (2) promoting mystical experiences in a "disproportionate way"; (3) carelessness in the use of prophecy; and (4) promoting the so-called "city church" teaching, through which Bickle, Jones and others suggested that all congregations in their city would one day be united under one governing eldership.

Sadly, the case of Bob Jones is no isolated incident in the history of the Pentecostal/charismatic movement. Unbridled mysticism has been common in many groups and has at times led to their demise. It also saps the spiritual energy out of churches, distracting believers from the priorities of biblical worship, godly living and evangelism. Self-proclaimed prophets and visionaries,

with all their high-minded talk of hearing audible directives from God, unknowingly steal for themselves the
glory due to Christ alone.

Charismatic Witchcraft: Manipulation through Mysticism

Witchcraft is not a practice that most people associate
with Christianity. The term invokes images of black cal-
drons, magic spells and satanic rituals—activities
Bible-believing Christians abhor. Nevertheless, if we de-
fine the term *witchcraft* properly, we can safely say that
many charismatic churches in America are filled with it.

Witchcraft (or sorcery) appears in a list of sins in Galatians 5 (contrasting with the fruit of the Spirit) that the
apostle Paul identifies as "deeds of the flesh." Also included in this list are sexual immorality, hatred, jeal-
ousy, selfish ambition and drunkenness. While we normally associate witchcraft with demonic spiritual forces,
Paul reminds us that it is a work of the flesh, a natural
byproduct of corrupt human nature.

Witchcraft can be defined as any effort on the part on
an individual to employ ungodly spiritual means to dominate, control or manipulate others. Manipulation in one
form or another occurs every day in corporate board-
rooms, in the halls of Congress, even among families.
Whenever a person seeking to control others uses deception to achieve his or her goal, it becomes witchcraft.

When witchcraft subtly invades charismatic churches,
the pattern is typical. A church member, usually a zealous and sincere Christian, is frustrated with the condition of his congregation. He may sense a lack of holiness, a shortage of corporate prayer or a need for
spiritual revival. As he shares his concerns with others

and prophesies out of his frustration, members of the congregation begin to elevate him as a special messenger from God. In order to live up to this status, he becomes more and more pious. He spends inordinate amounts of time in prayer or Bible study, shunning "frivolous" amusements. Although he may have numerous personal or financial problems, he becomes, in his own eyes, more spiritual than the church's leaders.

Because he has assigned himself a lofty degree of self-importance, he expects to receive messages from God regularly. He may begin to hear audible voices, see angels or simply receive regular "revelations" during prayer. Everything he does becomes spiritualized; every nighttime dream contains a message for the church. His aura of spirituality causes people to revere him. He is placed on a pedestal, from which he can bring havoc on the church.

Years ago I knew a woman who fit this description. The wife of a prominent Christian leader, she was one of the most spiritually minded people I have ever met. To this day I do not question her devotion to Jesus Christ. She was sincere about revival, yet so intense in her convictions that some people were afraid of her. This was partly because she was known to stand up at the appropriate moment during a church service and deliver a prophetic utterance that sent cold chills down the spines of everyone in attendance. Sometimes she shouted her message indignantly. Other times she wept softly and whispered. Whatever the case, most members of the congregation felt that this woman had a special relationship with God that afforded her access to "inside information" from heaven.

Her mysticism, as the years passed, grew more extreme. Once, in a late-night prayer meeting, she claimed to see an angel hovering nearby, brandishing a huge sword. Assuming that the appearance of this heavenly being was a signal of imminent revival, she staged nightly prayer vigils on the site and reported numerous other sightings of angels there. A few in the group said they saw them, too. Those of us who did not see them were told we lacked faith. The prayer meetings drew lots of curious seekers who wanted to see an angel for themselves. The revival did not occur.

Later this woman became convinced that our church had arrived at a critical juncture and that we all needed to commit ourselves to participate in daily prayer meetings. If we did not pray, she warned week after week, the Holy Spirit's anointing would leave us. Other leaders in the church, while increasingly disturbed by her dogmatism, took her advice seriously. Once, when she suspected that church members were disobeying God by not praying for revival every day, she prophesied to the church that God hated our worship and had rejected us.

I had walked in the grace of God for several years by that time and knew my heavenly Father did not treat His children so brutally, so I rejected this woman's message as false prophecy. But I did not realize how destructive false prophecy can be until I surveyed the damage a few months later. Many members were struggling emotionally and some questioned whether they were accepted in Christ. The elitist attitudes promoted by this woman's prophecies and revelations eventually brought division.

Throwing Mysticism Overboard

Charismatic churches that tolerate this kind of quirky mysticism are headed for trouble. Either they will self-destruct when church members grow weary of the constant madness, or a segment of the group will ultimately embrace deception and take on cultlike characteristics.

How can we guard against unhealthy mysticism while leaving room for the miraculous power of God? Pentecostal and charismatic groups have grappled with this issue for years.

Since the apostle Paul was well-acquainted with his own first-century version of "charismatic chaos," we do well to find the answer to this question in his first letter to the Corinthians, which contains the classic biblical treatise on the gifts of the Holy Spirit. We can derive four basic principles from the New Testament on this subject.

1. Spiritual gifts, properly used, always edify.

Since you are eager to have spiritual gifts, try to excel in gifts that build up the church.

1 Corinthians 14:12

True biblical prophecy, in the New Testament sense, has little to do with conjecture about the future, wars and rumors of wars, Armageddon or the next stock market crash. It may at times involve the foretelling of a future event, as when the prophet Agabus warned the church at Antioch of a coming famine (Acts 11:28). But such foretelling must always be for the purpose of edification, not to satisfy a base human desire for sensationalism. Too much of the so-called prophesying that goes on in charismatic churches today is a corruption of the real thing.

True prophecy is a message carrying the mark of God on it. It may come in the form of a sermon, but not all sermons can be classified as prophecies since not all preachers seek God earnestly for His message. It may come in the form of an utterance delivered by a church member during a worship service, but not all so-called prophecies given in charismatic services bear the mark of God on them, either.

Paul tells us that all true prophecy must edify. It must stir the church, not by human emotion or manipulation but by the anointing of the Spirit.

When a so-called prophet's message draws more attention to his own spirituality than to Jesus Christ and His purposes, we can be sure he is not employing the gift of the Holy Spirit. He is exercising his own vanity, trying to impress people by making them think he has a privileged connection to God.

2. False prophets are motivated by spiritual pride.

Did the word of God originate with you? . . . If anybody thinks he is a prophet or spiritually gifted, let him acknowledge that what I am writing to you is the Lord's command.

1 Corinthians 14:36-37

Paul told the Corinthians that prophets were to be subject to other prophets. He was reminding them that they were not a law unto themselves, spiritual Lone Rangers inventing their own doctrines. They were to submit themselves to one another in humility, rather, while holding each other accountable to adhere to the faith.

In Paul's day, the philosophy of gnosticism represented a major threat to the Church. Gnostics believed that salvation could be obtained by tapping into a secret source of divine knowledge reserved for an elite few. To this day this concept is promoted in charismatic churches. Some charismatic leaders boast of their discovery of "new" revelations that other Christians have not recognized. Whole churches sometimes adopt attitudes of superiority because they have embraced obscure doctrines about baptism, spiritual warfare or methods of prayer. They assume that their remarkable knowledge has set them on a higher plane than ordinary Christians.

But Paul warns us not to be misled by those who claim access to special revelation. In Colossians 2:18–19, he says that those who make such arrogant boasts have lost connection with the Head of the Church, the Lord Jesus Christ. There is no mysterious body of spiritual knowledge waiting to be revealed. God has unveiled His glorious purpose in His Son, and our salvation comes from faith in Him alone.

3. God is not the author of confusion.

Therefore, my brothers, be eager to prophesy, and do not forbid speaking in tongues. But everything should be done in a fitting and orderly way.

1 Corinthians 14:39-40

I was in a meeting once that involved congregations from several area churches in northern Virginia. Following a time of worship, a woman near the front of the auditorium began prophesying in a belligerent tone, condemning the congregation for our "disobedience" and peppering her message with *Thus says the Lord.* Her words did not edify, nor was the message prophetic, because it did not reflect the heart of God or offer any redemption.

A blanket of confusion and gloom dropped onto the congregation. People fidgeted anxiously in their seats. This woman claimed to speak for God but her words did not sound like the loving heavenly Father they all knew.

The non-Christians in the meeting, moreover, probably inferred that God was indeed a cruel taskmaster.

Thankfully, one of the local pastors attending the service approached the podium and corrected the woman in a gracious spirit. When he announced that her message was not a true word from God, I could feel everyone in the room breathe a palpable sigh of relief. In a split second, the uneasiness vanished. We all left the meeting that night reassured of God's love—not that God does not chasten His children through His servants the prophets, but that He does not scold us out of frustration or correct us without offering any hope.

False prophecies, regrettably, are not always corrected from the pulpit. Congregations subjected continually to this kind of confusion become prey for all kinds of spiritual and emotional problems. Pastors, as God-appointed shepherds of the flock, are responsible to protect their churches from such abuse.

4. More important than charismatic gifts is the fruit of the Spirit.

> If I speak in the tongues of men and of angels, but have not love, I am only a resounding gong or a clanging cymbal.
>
> 1 Corinthians 13:1

Certain Pentecostals and charismatics sustain a profound interest in securing spiritual power. Prophets promise to train Christians how to discern the future. Evangelists offer instruction in how to heal the sick. Some advertise their prowess in casting out demons, while others boast of having mastered the techniques of spiritual warfare over cities and nations.

Certainly we are exhorted in the Scriptures to desire spiritual gifts. But we have need for caution. Our main priority must be to manifest the nature of Christ to the world—not only by doing His works, but by showing His love.

It is time for all of us charismatics and Pentecostals to inspect what we have built over the last few decades. We must determine whether Christian character is the mark of our ministry and ask ourselves if love is at the heart of what we do. Our structures may be impressive and our numbers swelling. But it is possible we are simply making noise with gongs and cymbals, standing on a foundation of sand that can be washed away at any moment.

If we seek to demonstrate to the world the fruit of the Spirit, we can avoid that fate.

Fabricating the Anointing 8

Paul Cain needed no introduction when he stepped up to the podium at a large charismatic conference I was attending in San Antonio in December 1989. Everyone in the audience had heard the astounding stories of this man's prophetic prowess, and many in the crowd were hoping to see and hear his spiritual gifts in action that evening. The atmosphere was charged with nervous anticipation as Cain finished his sermon and began his practice of calling out individuals by name and delivering uniquely tailored "words from the Lord."

The nervousness was understandable. It was said that when Cain had spoken at a conference in 1988 sponsored by Vineyard Ministries International in Anaheim, California, a strange power surge had reportedly occurred, short-circuiting a video camera and telephone system. Many people attending that conference had taken this as a sign of the Holy Spirit's power, and Cain began to be viewed by some charismatics as a forerunner of a coming revival of New Testament-style signs, wonders and miracles. On several occasions Vineyard leader John Wimber touted him as such.

The stories circulating about Paul Cain set him in a class by himself. Prior to his birth, his sickly mother is said to have been visited by an angel who told her that her baby would grow up to preach the Gospel in the manner of the apostle Paul. She was subsequently healed of four major illnesses, according to Cain's oft-repeated testimony.

Cain typically told his audiences that at age eight he was visited by the same angel and commissioned to preach and heal the sick. From 1947 to 1958, he ministered in Pentecostal tent crusades during the heyday of revivalists Oral Roberts, William Branham and A. A. Allen. He was famous in certain circles for his reputed ability to identify by name perfect strangers in a crowd. He would often call people out, then proceed to name their secret transgressions. On one occasion, after astonishing a California congregation in this way, Cain reported that the pastor crawled under a pew and repented of his sins, gripped by fear that he might be exposed publicly as well.

Cain came to be viewed as a modern-day Nathan, pointing his finger at guilty sinners and hypocrites. But, because he was repulsed by the pride and greed associated with many healing ministries of the 1950s, Cain says he decided not to return to the pulpit until he identified "a new breed" of humble, young church leaders.

With all this background, none of us gathered at the San Antonio Convention Center knew quite what to expect. The lights might go out. Television cameras might blow up. A prominent pastor might be humiliated publicly. There might even be an earthquake, since a story was circulating that Cain had accurately predicted a minor trembler in southern California earlier that year. But whatever would transpire, most of us seated in the auditorium believed that Paul Cain was a special messenger from God equipped with divine power.

Nothing earthshaking took place that evening. After his sermon Cain delivered prophecies to about ten individuals or couples. Each of the messages was laced with bits of personal data—first names, cities, street numbers.

To one pastor and his wife, personal friends of mine, he mentioned the number 4001 (their church office was located on 4001 Newberry Road) and predicted that they would experience great revival in their Florida city. At another point Cain asked if "Mark and Debbie" from Washington, D.C., were in the audience. This couple had pastored a church in Washington for several years with a ministry office located at 139 C Street, near the U.S. Capitol. "There's something about 139 C," Cain said, and he proceeded to predict that spiritual revival would someday impact Capitol Hill.

Most people left the meeting that night astounded at the remarkable demonstration of the word of knowledge in Paul Cain's prophecies. It seemed that Cain had literally "read these people's mail" by recounting personal information he could not have known about total strangers. But I found myself struggling with what happened that night, despite my belief in the gifts of the Spirit.

I had no reason to doubt Cain's sincerity. He seemed like a humble man with a refreshing perspective. But it disturbed me that almost everyone who received these prophetic directives was part of the full-time staff of the ministry sponsoring the conference. It also seemed puzzling that all the information Cain ostensibly received from God was printed in a staff address directory that I knew was easily available to conference speakers. Surely Paul Cain would not have studied that list prior to the meeting, then "recalled" the names and numbers to make us think he had revelatory powers! I dismissed the thought.

A year later my questions resurfaced. If this man were a true prophet from God, most of his prophecies would be coming true, wouldn't they? I began to conduct my own research.

The majority of the personal messages Cain had conveyed that December evening in San Antonio, I discovered, had fallen to the ground. The church on 4001 Newberry Road, for example, had closed and most of the members had left the city, including the pastor and his wife. "Mark and Debbie" had resigned their pastoral positions in Washington, D.C., the 139 C Street office was rented out to another group and the church had moved to the suburbs. Another young man—who had been told by Cain that he would orchestrate a fruitful ministry in southern California—told me he had moved to Texas and had no desire ever to live in California again.

A year after the San Antonio meeting, I interviewed Paul Cain. He insisted during our conversation that no one has ever proved that he obtains information from any source other than God. Two years later I asked him to explain why these prophecies did not come true. I also asked him if he had seen any information about those people's addresses before he prophesied over them. He would not answer my questions directly, but through a friend denied any wrongdoing.

I have found no evidence to suggest that Paul Cain is a swindler or impostor. In terms of lifestyle, he lives modestly, and several prominent leaders in the charismatic renewal endorse his ministry and vouch for his character. But I cannot ignore the fact that most of the prophecies he gave in that meeting in 1989 were inaccurate. As I have struggled to reconcile this situation, I have reached one important conclusion. We are treading on dangerous ground if we build our lives naively on the words of any man or woman who claims to speak for God.

We charismatics are prone to deifying human beings. If someone occasionally experiences the gift of miracles in his ministry, we want to make him into a god. The people of Lystra decided that Paul and Barnabas were gods because they had healed a lame man (Acts 14:11–12), and the residents of Malta said the same of Paul because God healed him of a deadly snakebite (Acts 28:6). In both cases Paul rejected the suggestion and insisted he was only a man. Today, I fear, some church leaders are not so quick to dismiss it when they are mistaken for deity.

Billy Graham is not one of these. But as much as I respect him—I love his sermons and consider him a champion of Christian integrity—I do not think he is without flaws, nor do I expect every word he utters to be divinely inspired. Why, then, should we expect perfection of Paul Cain or any other so-called Christian prophet?

Even if Paul Cain did receive information supernaturally from God during that meeting in San Antonio, there was something dangerous operating in the convention hall that night. Thousands of Christians had put Cain on a pedestal where no man or woman belongs. People expected him almost to be like God. It was a setup for disappointment.

Stripping Away the Facade

Charismatics tend to boast that we proclaim the Gospel of Christ not only in words but in power. But the sad truth is, some of our power is little more than an illusion.

I have already mentioned the television news show "Prime Time Live" that conducted an investigation in 1991 into three Pentecostal evangelists based in Texas. They charged that the men were defrauding their audiences and mishandling ministry funds. One segment of the program focused on faith healer W. V. Grant, pastor of the 4,000-member Eagle's Nest Family Church in Dallas.

ABC reporters taped footage of one of Grant's healing services in which the preacher prayed for an elderly black man seated near an aisle. After pulling him out of his seat, Grant tossed the man's walking cane triumphantly across the room and urged him to walk around the auditorium. The crowd cheered, obviously assuming that the man had been healed of an ambulatory problem.

Such was not the case. After the incident, when the "healed" man walked into the vestibule of the church, ABC reporters asked him to describe his experience. He told them innocently that he did not have a problem with his legs but with an ailment in his arm, which he said still bothered him. When asked about the cane, he explained that it belonged to the woman seated next to him.

I do not intend, by citing this apparent misrepresentation, to be backing investigative journalists against charismatic ministry or against any and all supernatural manifestations. (Far from it!) "Prime Time Live," moreover, has been charged with distortion and misrepresentation in that very broadcast (apart from the man who was not healed of a walking problem). What I am saying, rather, is that illusion *does* play a role, unfortunately, in many charismatic healing services.

I have often watched as numbers of people stream to the altar after a minister identifies their particular infirmity by a "word of knowledge." In most cases, the sicknesses that are "healed" are undocumentable: headaches, ringing in the ears, stomach ailments. The person who arrives at the meeting in a wheelchair, meanwhile, usually leaves the service disappointed, feeling that God cares less for him than for the woman healed of migraines.

I would like to pose the possibility that if God's power is not obvious at such a meeting, and if the results are not verifiable, *then a genuine healing anointing may not be present.* If the power of Christ is poured out in a service, on the other hand, surely more will occur than the healing of a few sore throats. And when we reduce the power of God to that level, are we not belittling it and limiting God Himself, both by expecting healings to occur only during church meetings (most healings recorded in Scripture occurred more spontaneously) and by expecting only "minor" healings?

Every time Jesus healed the sick, it was not staged or contrived and it was indisputably a miracle, a sign producing awe and reverence in those who witnessed it. This was also true when the apostles proclaimed the Gospel throughout the Roman world "with signs following." The blind received their sight, deaf ears were opened and the crippled took up their pallets and walked.

These kinds of miracles still happen today. But they do not occur at the hands of so-called faith healers who manipulate their audiences with theatrics and outright sleight of hand.

Two sons of Aaron under the Old Covenant were struck dead because they offered "strange fire" in the Tabernacle while performing their priestly duties (Leviticus 10:1-2). The tragic end of Nadab and Abihu should convince us not to tamper with the anointing of God. The Holy Spirit is not ours to manipulate. We must not mix the fire of the Spirit with our own impure (if sweet-smelling) agenda. I wonder if those who do so do not disqualify themselves from the ministry.

Falling Down "Under the Power"

Perhaps the most familiar way to fabricate the anointing occurs when people are "slain in the Spirit." The practice of slumping onto the floor after receiving prayer, usually into the waiting arms of a "catcher," has become standard in some charismatic churches.

Let me be quick to add that this phenomenon can represent a legitimate touch from the Holy Spirit. In view of the power and sovereignty of God, to deny it would be foolish.

Francis MacNutt, a long-time leader in the renewal and one of the foremost authorities on Christian healing, believes that falling under the power can be an extraordinary demonstration of God's power, an intimate experience of His presence, an impetus to repentance or deliverance from evil spirits, and an environment for healing. "I find that resting in the Spirit," he writes, "is a marvelous ministry gift that often leads people to experience the love of Jesus, lasting healing and deliverance."[1]

At the same time, this phenomenon can be and often is faked. And it is the counterfeit that we should deplore.

One of the few incidents in the first-century Church resembling falling under the power is the account of Ananias and Sapphira, except that they were literally slain by the Spirit (Acts 5:1–11)! They fell, however, because the Holy Spirit convicted them of sin, not because they were healed or anointed for ministry. Demon-possessed people often fell down in the presence of Jesus and His disciples (Luke 4:35; Mark 9:26). The unconverted Saul fell to his knees when he saw the heavenly vision of Christ on the road to Damascus (Acts 9:4, 22:7). And John, the beloved disciple, fell "as though dead" in the presence of the risen Lord Jesus (Revelation 1:17).

But collapsing under the power of God in the early Church was not common among believers. Nor does the Bible record anyone swooning or falling down unconscious after receiving prayer for healing. When Jesus touched the sick with His hand, cast out a demon with His word or instructed the lame to get up and walk, infirmities were cured visibly—but nowhere accompanied by fainting.

When the Holy Spirit descended on the first disciples at Pentecost, the men and women in the Upper Room spoke in tongues and heard the sound of a rushing wind but no one is recorded to have "fallen under the power." The writers of the New Testament practiced the laying on of hands for both healing and ordination (1 Timothy 4:14, 5:22). But nowhere in the epistles does a New Testament writer tell us to expect people to fall to the ground when we lay hands on them.

Why, then, is being slain in the Spirit so common today? God undoubtedly chooses to touch some individuals in this remarkable way. But another reason is apparent: It is a learned behavior, a tradition passed down from Pentecostal forerunners like Maria Woodworth-Etter and from healing evangelists like the flamboyant Kathryn Kuhlman.

In the ministry of Woodworth-Etter in the Midwest in the late 1800s, people reportedly "struck down by the power of God" were considered to be under profound conviction of sin. (The same was true in the ministries of John Wesley, Jonathan Edwards, Charles G. Finney and others.)

When charismatics are slain in the Spirit, however, it seldom has to do with conviction. It is generally interpreted as a human response to the anointing of the Holy Spirit, especially relating to healing. Kuhlman called it "the blessing." Often in her services, hundreds of people fell down simultaneously at a wave of her hand.

Today, falling under the power is often considered an experience that should be sought for its own sake.

Many is the time I have stood in a line of people and waited for a Pentecostal evangelist to anoint me or pray for healing. In almost every case, the minister placed a sweaty palm on my forehead and began to nudge me backward. Once, when I refused to go limp and drop into a catcher's arms, the evangelist rebuked me mildly, saying, "Don't resist the Spirit." When it became clear that I was not going to join my friends on the floor, he moved over to the person on my left and began to pray for him, pushing him gently until he collapsed. I have also watched evangelists send believers tumbling to the floor by brute force, by whacking them on the forehead.

Putting on a Good Charismatic Show

Pushing people to the ground to simulate God's anointing is a sham that cheapens the gifts of the Holy Spirit. But it is not usually the minister who is guilty of this unfortunate fabrication. In most cases I have observed, it is the person being prayed for who is fabricating the anointing, pretending to be slain. I have watched men, women and children as they relax on the floor after being "felled" in charismatic services. Many of the women discreetly straighten their skirts, their eyes still closed, while others peek at the audience. They are not "under the power." They are helping to create an illusion.

Particularly tragic about this typical scenario is the fact that these people who have been "slain in the Spirit" believe the experience has some lasting spiritual effect. At one charismatic church I attended, I sat through a three-hour session consisting mainly of bodies falling (or being pushed) onto a carpeted area near the stage. When the meeting concluded, I overheard people saying to each other, "Wasn't that exciting! God really moved tonight."

These comments grieved me. Nothing profound had been preached from the Scriptures. No one had been converted or healed, although a few said they felt God touch them. Nor did I get the impression that the people who spent so much time on the floor that evening were convicted of sin or leaving the meeting more burdened for the lost. It was almost as if we were putting on a show— but whom were we entertaining?

On the other side of it, I talked with a Pentecostal evangelist from New Zealand several years ago who had been encouraging spiritual revival in that nation. He told how a group of Christian young people had visited a Methodist church in Auckland to encourage the believers there. The Methodists were not charismatic and had no previous experience with Pentecostal practices. Yet when the evangelist preached his sermon on repentance and revival, some of the members of the congregation literally fell to the floor and began weeping and confessing their sins. Such a scenario is a genuine expression of the power of God.

Slaying in the Spirit can be employed as a means to manipulate a crowd. If dozens of people collapse in succession like dominos when a preacher waves his arm over an audience, he is perceived as an anointed vessel of God's power and his ministry is thus legitimized. But what basis is there in Scripture for throwing the anointing of God around in an auditorium so that people can receive healing en masse or achieve an emotional high?

If Jesus had waved His arm over the crowds seated on the hillsides of Galilee and caused them to swoon, I am sure the writers of the Gospels would have mentioned the miracle. But Jesus did not perform signs and wonders to excite crowds or cause goose bumps. He preached the truth and met physical needs.

Discerning Between True and False Anointings

Genuine miracles have a profound impact. Moses needed only one burning bush experience in the desert before agreeing to deliver his fellow Jews out of Egyptian bondage. Somehow we charismatics have adopted the notion that miraculous signs and wonders are supposed to occur at the drop of a hat or on a daily basis.

Why else are we misled by almost anyone claiming to have an anointing from God? Are we so anxious to witness miracles that, reluctant to test for the real thing (which might show a "lack of faith"), we are willing to settle for a counterfeit? Surely we do not honestly believe we can further Christ's Kingdom with forgery and deceit. The apostle Paul warned us to be careful how we build the Kingdom of God:

> For no one can lay any foundation other than the one already laid, which is Jesus Christ. If any man builds on this foundation using gold, silver, costly stones, wood, hay or straw, his work will be shown for what it is, because the Day will bring it to light. It will be revealed with fire, and the fire will test the quality of each man's work.
>
> 1 Corinthians 3:11–13

We who identify with the charismatic renewal would do well to examine the quality of what all of us together have been building for the past thirty years. Although ultimately it is only the Lord who judges our work, it is obvious that much of what we have erected in recent years has been of shoddy construction. In many cases the poor quality has resulted from inferior building materials—the wood, hay and stubble of false prophecies, fabricated anointings, exaggerated claims and empty boasting. If we want to build something permanent, it must be grounded in Christ, designed according to His Word and fashioned with integrity.

Jesus warned His disciples that charlatans would use gifts as a disguise while they preyed upon the naïve:

> "Watch out for false prophets. They come to you in sheep's clothing, but inwardly they are ferocious wolves. By their fruit you will recognize them. . . . Not everyone who says to me, 'Lord, Lord,' will enter the kingdom of heaven, but only he who does the will of my Father who is in heaven. Many will say to me on that day, 'Lord, Lord, did we not prophesy in your name, and in your name drive out demons and perform many miracles?' Then I will tell them plainly, 'I never knew you. Away from me, you evildoers!'"
>
> Matthew 7:15–16, 21–23

Outwardly false prophets bear an amazing resemblance to the real thing. But on the inside, Jesus said, they are "ferocious wolves," and their hidden motive is to steal money or attention from the flock of God.

Jesus did not say these men actually healed the sick or cast out demons. They simply *claimed* that they performed such miracles in order to attract a following, and the possibility exists that they did not. It is no different today. The charismatic movement in America has produced its share of pretenders. Plenty of so-called Spirit-filled evangelists have mastered the art of shouting, "Thus says the Lord!" They prophesy with eloquence and the proper intonation, but their message is a sham.

Others use deception to convince audiences of their divine giftings.

Jesus did not offer His warning to make us suspicious of healing or other spiritual gifts. He Himself healed the sick and performed miracles, and His disciples raised the dead by God's power. If we believe the message of the New Testament, then we will accept prophecy, miracles and healings (as recorded in 1 Corinthians 12) as genuine expressions of the Holy Spirit's anointing.

No, Jesus' warning in Matthew 7 was not intended to scare us away from the gifts of the Spirit. He was alerting us to the fact that impostors will attempt to hide their true motives behind a facade of spirituality, and He was exhorting us to use discernment.

We do well do follow His exhortation.

Merchandising the Anointing

After persecution scattered Christ's disciples throughout Judea and Samaria, a significant evangelistic breakthrough occurred among the Samaritans the chronicler Luke tells us. Large crowds gathered in a dusty little town to hear Philip the evangelist preach the Gospel, and the villagers witnessed miraculous signs and wonders confirming his account of the resurrection of the Son of God. "Evil spirits came out of many," according to Luke's account, "and many paralytics and cripples were healed" (Acts 8:7). It was one of the earliest miracle crusades of the first-century Church. But it was not without its problems. During that initial missionary outreach, the Gospel was challenged by a charlatan for the first time. Simon was his name and conning the public was his game. Even without the modern-day benefits of direct mail marketing and cable television, Simon the sorcerer, also known as "the Great Power," amassed quite a following among the local townspeople. It must have come as a shock to all of Samaria when this powerful, New Age-style guru announced that he, too, had decided to be baptized and become a disciple of Jesus Christ.

But Simon, we are told, had a wicked heart. He was full of greed and lusted for the attention of the crowds. He watched in amazement as his former followers, who had once trusted in his quack cures, were healed supernaturally and permanently of their diseases by the power of God. Simon was overcome by his self-centered appetite for the crowd's approval. Luke writes:

> When Simon saw that the Spirit was given at the laying on of the apostles' hands, he offered them money and said, "Give me also this ability so that everyone on whom I lay my hands may receive the Holy Spirit."
>
> Peter answered: "May your money perish with you, because you thought you could buy the gift of God with money! You have no part or share in this ministry, because your heart is not right before God. Repent of this wickedness and pray to the Lord. Perhaps he will forgive you for having such a thought in your heart. For I see that you are full of bitterness and captive to sin."
>
> Acts 8:18–23

Never again in the New Testament do we hear of Simon. But we have heard of men just like him down through history—men who made an initial commitment to follow Christ but who later betrayed Him by attempting to use the Gospel for personal gain. Charismatic and Pentecostal churches in this century have produced their share of Simons. Some of them likely set out from the beginning to take advantage of God's people. Most of them, I suspect, began their ministry careers in earnest but later allowed themselves to be corrupted by the love of money.

Peter told Simon the sorcerer that he could have "no part or share in this ministry" because of his covetousness (Acts 8:21). Greed, in other words, was enough to disqualify Simon from standing among Christ's disciples. This theme is repeated often in the New Testament epistles. In delineating the qualifications of a church leader, Paul states that the candidate must not be "a lover of money" (1 Timothy 3:3). He specifies in another list of eligibility requirements for church elders that men in such roles must not be "pursuing dishonest gain" (Titus 1:7). Peter exhorts church leaders in this way:

> Be shepherds of God's flock that is under your care, serving as overseers—not because you must, but because you are willing, as God wants you to be; not greedy for money, but eager to serve.
>
> 1 Peter 5:2

Many charismatics and Pentecostals in America, sadly, have either twisted these biblical passages intentionally or simply overlooked them. We have not been on our guard against the charlatan. Just as Simon the sorcerer attempted to buy the power of God so he could sell it and make himself rich, so corrupt men and women today have used the name of Christ to gain wealth and recognition.

The Profiteers of God

In 1992 Hollywood released a feature film about a religious con artist named Jonas Nightingale. The movie, *Leap of Faith*, starred comedian Steve Martin as the cunning preacher who knew how to manipulate Christians in order to get at their wallets. He was the stereotypical huckster, better at preying than praying. The Rev. Nightingale staged an old-fashioned tent revival in a Kansas town, advertised his meetings all over the county and wowed his Pentecostal audiences every night with his miraculous ability to identify people suffering from specific ailments.

Behind the stage Nightingale had an assistant who sent him messages through a tiny electronic earphone. The preacher was not receiving divine messages from God, nor was he healing anyone, but he knew how to create the illusion that lame people could walk. The people were convinced Jonas Nightingale was an anointed man of God. And every night the townsfolk who attended his "revival" services stuffed the offering buckets with what the evangelist was really after: lots of cash.

There will always be Jonas Nightingales for us to watch out for, but most of the corruption and trickery going on in charismatic churches today is far more subtle than the Hollywood version. In actuality, the leaders who are best at manipulating audiences and collecting big offerings are not the outsiders who blow into town with dark sunglasses and criminal records. They are trusted men and women of God who have been enticed over the years by greed.

When Jim Bakker started his broadcast ministry in the early 1960s, he wanted (like many zealous preachers) to reach the world for Christ. But apparently he allowed himself to be deceived by a lust for riches. Years later, after he had spent many months in federal prison for defrauding his followers, he wrote a letter from his cell, which his daughter mailed to his supporters in June 1992. It included this confession:

> Many today believe that the evidence of God's blessing on them is a new car, a new house, a good job, and riches, etc. But that is far from the truth of God's Word. If that be the case, then gambling casino owners and drug kingpins and movie stars are blessed of God. Jesus did not teach that riches were a sign of God's blessings. In fact, Jesus said,

"It is hard for a rich man to enter the kingdom of Heaven."
And he talked about the "deceitfulness of riches."

I have spent many months reading every word Jesus
spoke. I wrote them out over and over, and I read them
over and over again. There is no way, if you take the
whole counsel of God's Word, that you can equate riches
or material things as a sign of God's blessing.

Jesus said, "Blessed are the poor in spirit (humble),
blessed are those who mourn, who are meek, who hunger
and thirst for righteousness. Blessed are the merciful,
the pure in heart, the peacemakers, those who are persecuted, reviled, and spoken of falsely for Christ's sake."

I have asked God to forgive me and I ask all who have
sat under my ministry to forgive me for preaching a
gospel emphasizing earthly prosperity. Jesus said, "Do
not lay up for yourselves treasures on earth." He wants
us to be in love with Him. . . . If we equate earthly possessions and earthly relationships with God's favor, what
do we tell the billions of those living in poverty, or what
do you do if depression hits, or what do you say to those
who lose a loved one?[1]

Since Bakker was sentenced to a lengthy prison term,
other prominent leaders have distanced themselves
from the prosperity message. In 1993 healing evangelist Benny Hinn stunned some of his followers when he
announced that he was washing his hands of the so-
called "prosperity gospel." Hinn told his church, Orlando
Christian Center, as well as *Charisma* magazine and a
Trinity Broadcasting Network audience, that he no
longer believed that message was from God.

What convinced him? Hinn said he came to the conclusion while he was conducting healing crusades in
Asia. God would not permit him, he said, to stand before the poverty-stricken people of Manila and promise
them that if they gave in the offering, God would bless
them with more money. If the prosperity message should

not be preached in the Philippines, Hinn decided, it should not be preached in America. "It is not a message from God," he said.

The saddest part of this story is that it took this long for many of us to realize the true origins of this gospel of greed.

The Deceitfulness of Riches

Benny Hinn was not the first charismatic leader to recognize that our movement has been poisoned by an unholy emphasis on wealth and success. Years before the Jim Bakker/PTL scandal, many believers in America were so repulsed by money-grubbing TV preachers that they returned to their denominational churches in disgust.

It is easy to place blame for this travesty. We could blame the proponents of the prosperity gospel and say it was all caused by faulty theology. In his 1993 book *Christianity in Crisis*, cult specialist Hank Hanegraaff compiled enough evidence to indict half-a-dozen Word-faith preachers for tampering with Scripture and spreading faulty doctrines. But if American church audiences had not already had itching ears eager to embrace the gospel of instant health and wealth, it would never have become such big business in the U.S.

The prosperity gospel is not so much a theological problem as it is a heart problem. Those who twist Scripture to say that Jesus was rich, that His disciples had a condominium in Capernaum or that God owes you a Mercedes-Benz are simply trying to justify their own covetousness. Rather than try to adjust their faulty theology, we should simply recognize that these men are corrupt and we should reject their message, lest we too be tricked by the deceitfulness of riches.

As we charismatics attempt to get our own house in order, I hope we will remove all traces of this corruption. How can we be sure that the love of money is not corrupting our churches and ministries? Here are three danger signals that can alert us to the presence of a charlatan:

1. Beware of shepherds who do not feed their sheep.

Covetous people care for no one but themselves. When the deceitfulness of riches grips a person's heart, it prevents him or her from caring for others or expressing genuine compassion. This is why the Bible says that a church leader who loves money is disqualified from serving the people of God. His heart cannot possibly be a channel of God's love.

A pastor I know of was often asked to travel to various cities during the week to preach in special crusades. A dynamic speaker, he got lots of these invitations. Every time he preached, the church handed him an honorarium check, sometimes in excess of $3,000 or $4,000. In some cases they also handed him a wad of cash that had been put into the offering plate after the check had been written.

This evangelist often took the cash and headed to his favorite men's clothing shop. He admitted to his closest associates that he had a special affection for nice things, and he was known to spend up to $400 on belts and ties during one shopping spree. He spent many times that amount on gold and diamond jewelry.

Is this where money from a church offering plate belongs? Certainly ministers deserve to be supported generously for their services. But it does not require a supernatural gift of discernment to determine whether a man or woman of God has crossed the line into materialistic excess. If Christians would stop defending ministers who lead such lifestyles, we might see a return to biblical holiness among our church leaders.

The Lord sent a stern rebuke through the prophet Ezekiel to church leaders who insist on fleecing the flock for their own benefit. Though it was directed at the Jewish priests of apostate Israel, it applies to any contemporary pastor or evangelist who aims to get rich off of the people of God:

> "Son of man, prophesy against the shepherds of Israel; prophesy and say to them: 'This is what the Sovereign LORD says: Woe to the shepherds of Israel who only take care of themselves! Should not shepherds take care of the flock? You eat the curds, clothe yourselves with the wool and slaughter the choice animals, but you do not take care of the flock. You have not strengthened the weak or healed the sick or bound up the injured. You have not brought back the strays or searched for the lost. You have ruled them harshly and brutally. So they were scattered because there was no shepherd, and when they were scattered they became food for all the wild animals. . . .
>
> "'This is what the Sovereign LORD says: I am against the shepherds and will hold them accountable for my flock. I will remove them from tending the flock so that the shepherds can no longer feed themselves. I will rescue my flock from their mouths, and it will no longer be food for them.'"
>
> Ezekiel 34:1–5, 10

God obviously has strong feelings about shepherds who care more for themselves than the sheep that have been entrusted to their care. We should be just as protective, speaking out when we see a church leader falling into the trap of materialism.

2. Beware of any church leader whose message seems money-centered.

The Bible has plenty to say about money: how to save it, how to spend it, how to invest it, how to give it away. There is a legitimate need for Christians to learn biblical principles of money management, and churches often struggle because their members have never learned the biblical basis for tithing.

But the prosperity gospel, at its core, has little to do with biblical principles. On the contrary, it has been used as a means of manipulation—a way to entice people to give their money to someone so he can stuff his wallet.

Many of the principles taught by the prosperity preachers are sound doctrine. The Bible says clearly, for example, "Give, and it will be given to you. A good measure, pressed down, shaken together and running over, will be poured into your lap. For with the measure you use, it will be measured to you" (Luke 6:38).

The essence of this passage is obvious: God wants us to be generous. Jesus' instructions are to encourage us to display an attitude of cheerful sharing rather than hold tightly to our worldly possessions. Giving releases us to trust the Father for His abundant provision. But this verse is often manipulated to entice people to put large sums of money into an offering plate or direct mail envelope. It has even been made into a formula: If you give Amount A and you are using enough faith, God will multiply it into Amount B.

But the prosperity preachers have conveniently left out some of Jesus' other teachings on giving, especially His admonition in Matthew 6:1–4:

> "Be careful not to do your 'acts of righteousness' before men, to be seen by them. If you do, you will have no reward from your Father in heaven.

"So when you give to the needy, do not announce it
with trumpets, as the hypocrites do in the synagogues
and on the streets, to be honored by men. I tell you the
truth, they have received their reward in full. But when
you give to the needy, do not let your left hand know what
your right hand is doing, so that your giving may be in
secret."

So much of what occurs in charismatic churches in
the name of faith has been nothing more than self-con-
gratulatory trumpet-blowing—bragging in public about
our sacrifices to God when He says that giving is a holy
act to be done in secret. Because we have blown our
trumpets so loudly and made money a central part of
our message, many worship services resemble boister-
ous sales rallies. The love of money has tainted our
praise. It has caused many of us to shift our focus from
the spiritual to the material and assume that all God's
blessings are in the material realm.

The devil himself must have engineered this, since he
is a master at luring us to focus our attention on the
things of the flesh rather than the things of the Spirit.
If we were more discerning, we would have noticed early
on what a hollow ring the prosperity message produced.

But many of us were deceived by that hollow sound.
Today we face the challenge of removing this corruption
from our midst and preaching a purified message free
from greed and idolatry.

3. Reject those who take the Lord's name in vain.

The third Commandment prohibits us from taking
the Lord's name in vain. Yet there are evangelists and
church leaders who misuse the Lord's name every day
when they raise money. One of America's most notori-
ous televangelists spends up to 80 percent of his air time
urging his viewers to make "$1,000 vows of faith" to his

ministry. He claims that God will rescue his listeners from debt, poverty or failed businesses if they will become obedient givers.

During his syndicated TV program, this evangelist peers into the camera and claims to discern the specific needs of people in his viewing audience. "I see a businessman," the evangelist says. "You're sitting in your hotel room, discouraged about how your business is going. I see a housewife at home. You're so tired of not having enough to pay the bills." Then he explains how it works: "Send me your money and God will bless you. Operators are standing by. You can even put the bill on your MasterCard or Visa."

This man has crossed into dangerous territory. He claims to speak for God, sometimes even prophesying in the name of Christ, while his motive is apparent: to entice his listeners to send him their money. Despite the many missions projects this evangelist funds, the whole nation learned about his extravagant lifestyle in 1991 when a national news program investigated his fund-raising methods.

When it comes to how we treat other people's money, we charismatics need a fresh dose of the fear of God. It borders on blasphemy when church leaders stand in the pulpit and say with an air of authority, "God has told me that ten people in the audience are to give $2,000 each," or (even worse), "God is saying that those who give in this offering will receive a hundredfold return." How can we have the audacity to make such presumptuous, manipulative statements?

A list of such gimmicks would be endless. One of the most common is used in direct mail promotions sent by various ministries. In the fund-raising letter, the evangelist asks his supporters to write their prayer requests on a special card, which also includes a place to write in the amount of a designated gift. Somewhere in his letter, the evangelist implies that those who send back their prayer request with money will obtain an instant answer from God.

Is this any different from the medieval practice of buying indulgences from the Catholic Church?

The only way this sad state of affairs can be corrected is for those of us in the pews to demand a higher level of integrity on the part of our leaders. We must demand that the biblical standard be upheld: Greed is grounds for disqualification from church leadership.

Abusing Others with the Anointing

When Jorge Serrano Elias was elected president of Guatemala in 1991, he was heralded as the first democratically elected evangelical to head a government in Latin America. His election was seen as a signal that the rapidly growing evangelical population in Guatemala was now large enough to make a major impact in a Catholic-dominated country.

But President Serrano, a Pentecostal who prayed publicly at state events and talked privately about sharing the Gospel with Cuban leader Fidel Castro, proved a disappointment, both to the Christians in Guatemala who elected him and to the evangelical community around the world who had seen him as a trend-setter. In 1993, in an effort to root out corruption, Serrano dissolved the Congress, seized control of the press and rallied the military to support his self-coup. But Guatemala's Supreme Court condemned his actions, as did the international community. Within a week he was forced to flee the country. Serrano had followed in the footsteps of countless Latin American leaders before him: He had become a dictator.

Why did everyone, including Guatemala's evangelicals, condemn Serrano's seizure of power? Because it is impossible to reconcile Christianity with dictatorship, and Serrano had apparently tried to mix two opposing ideas—democracy and autocratic rule. International Christians hope his failure taught his peers that Christian heads of state must leave the power in the hands of the people.

But Serrano's ouster sent another message: Christians can be dictators. Sadly, charismatic churches in the U.S. have accommodated Christian dictatorship. Many of our leaders wield absolute power while most of us, unfamiliar with the principles of godly church government, neglect to challenge their governing style.

The apostle Peter laid down a set of guidelines for church leadership when he wrote his first epistle to the early Church:

> To the elders among you, I appeal as a fellow elder, a witness of Christ's sufferings and one who also will share in the glory to be revealed: Be shepherds of God's flock that is under your care, serving as overseers—not because you must, but because you are willing, as God wants you to be; not greedy for money, but eager to serve; not lording it over those entrusted to you, but being examples to the flock.
>
> 1 Peter 5:1–3

We lord it over others naturally. That is the way of the world. But Peter reminded the believers in Asia Minor that Christ had introduced a revolutionary new approach—leadership through humility, servanthood and example. Jesus demonstrated that radical approach to leadership when He dressed like a slave and washed His disciples' feet. When two of His closest followers entertained a lust for power, Jesus told them,

"You know that the rulers of the Gentiles lord it over them, and their high officials exercise authority over them. Not so with you. Instead, whoever wants to become great among you must be your servant, and whoever wants to be first must be your slave—just as the Son of Man did not come to be served, but to serve, and to give his life as a ransom for many."

Matthew 20:25–28

This godly method of governing, however, has not been the rule in most charismatic churches, particularly independent ones. Since the renewal blossomed in the late 1960s, many groups that began with vibrant faith degenerated quickly into legalism and authoritarianism. Some ministry leaders have exalted themselves as kings over their own kingdoms, giving their churches or ministries the characteristics of cults.

Spiritual Abuse

Keith was barely eighteen in 1970 when he got involved in the House of Bread, a charismatic prayer group that met on Saturday nights in a rustic cabin in northern Virginia, just ten miles outside of Washington, D.C. Like many other young people affected by the Jesus movement, Keith was eager to serve the Lord and give his energies to winning his friends to Christ.

The House of Bread was a healthy place to do that. The worship was rich, the Bible study enlightening and the friendships deep. The prayer group soon became an officially organized church, and at the age of twenty Keith was recognized as an elder. Jim, an older man with an Assemblies of God background, pastored the church and took Keith under his wing.

But trouble was brewing. In its formative years the House of Bread became aligned with the discipleship movement and the "Fort Lauderdale Five" (mentioned in chapter 1)—Derek Prince, Charles Simpson, Don Basham, Bob Mumford and Ern Baxter. Because these men had hammered out a special covenant among themselves, submitting their lives and ministries to one another, they taught that all Christians, in order to grow spiritually, should likewise submit themselves to a personal pastor or "shepherd."

The shepherding movement, like many Christian fads, swept through the Church and was embraced in varying degrees by many charismatic groups. Critics warned that Scripture does not encourage believers to depend on their pastors or spiritual "overseers" for daily guidance, and the movement was opposed by a few prominent voices in the Church, including Pat Robertson and Jack Hayford, as heresy.

But for Keith, the shepherding message seemed sound biblically, and he longed for the kind of close-knit covenant relationships that Prince, Simpson, Basham, Mumford and Baxter shared. Keith was eager to submit his life to Jim because he had so much to learn. And since Jim tended to be easygoing, Keith knew he would not expect him to come for advice every time he needed to make a personal decision.

Not everyone involved in the discipleship movement fared so well. In some churches members were told where they should be employed and what kind of furniture they should buy for their homes.

But Keith became a casualty of the movement after more than a decade when he began to register complaints about how the church was operated. He was paid a generous salary, and two other senior pastors were paid even more, but it bothered Keith that information about the pastors' salaries and benefits was not made available to the congregation. The budget was hidden because the church leaders did not feel the people had a right to know.

After raising questions about this autocratic management style, Keith was labeled a rebel and resigned. Jim, to whom he had looked for spiritual direction for more than twelve years, announced to the congregation that Keith was under the influence of Satan.

It took years for Keith and his wife to recover from the emotional devastation they experienced in the discipleship movement, though their experience was relatively mild. Part of their healing came when the Fort Lauderdale Five broke up and went their separate ways, most of them acknowledging that their teaching had been in error.

In 1989 Bob Mumford issued a formal apology to the Body of Christ, repenting for spreading teaching that caused so much abuse. His statement said, in part, that the shepherding movement had encouraged "an unhealthy submission resulting in perverse and unbiblical obedience to human leaders." Mumford then expressed regret: "Many of these abuses occurred within the spheres of my own responsibility. For the injury and shame caused to people, families and the larger Body of Christ, I repent with sorrow and ask for your forgiveness."[1]

In a subsequent interview with *Ministries Today* editor Jamie Buckingham, Mumford admitted that the shepherding emphasis was heresy. "I now see the biblical warnings, 'Don't lord it over the flock.' But I did. In my own heart, I got this triumphant feeling of being in charge. People, on the other hand, felt handled and pressured. We wrongly gave the impression you could not fellowship with any of us unless you did things our way. And that was wrong."[2]

That same year Maranatha Ministries (the campus evangelism group with which I was affiliated and which I wrote about in chapter 1) disbanded after its leaders recognized their own errors relating to authoritarianism. Maranatha's founder, Bob Weiner, issued a public apology. Church members had made inordinate personal sacrifices so that the group could succeed. Some put their careers on hold to support the local church. Others chose to forgo marriage because they feared they might compromise their standards by marrying someone outside Maranatha. Loyalty to the ministry had been stressed to the point of blacklisting people who left. The demise of Maranatha was fast, but it would take years for some Maranatha disciples to recover from the spiritual abuse they encountered during their years of association with the group.

And while Bob Weiner and various Maranatha leaders orchestrated some significant evangelistic breakthroughs on dozens of American university campuses, the ministry left a trail of wounded people. Abuses ranged from absurd to painful. Because Maranatha pastors were expected to groom their disciples to look their best, overweight people were reported to the ministry's headquarters and their names placed on a list. Several times a year their pastors were required to report on their weight loss progress. At one point, the ministry's elders threatened to excommunicate anyone who refused to get in shape.

Bob Weiner held the reins of power for the group like an autocrat, accountable to no one. His word was law and he trained his top leaders to rule in the same iron-fisted manner. Maranatha leaders were skilled in using Scripture to encourage loyalty, and anyone who balked at the idea of "total commitment" to the group was judged guilty of harboring a spirit of rebellion. Anyone brave enough to ask questions was accused of having a demon of intellectualism. Those courageous enough to leave the group were considered spiritually inferior.

Warning Signs

The only way we can root out authoritarianism from our churches is by teaching Christians to recognize the difference between godly and ungodly leadership. For too long charismatics have tolerated bad leaders and embraced for ourselves their flawed philosophy of governing by manipulation. Rather than servanthood in our churches, we have encouraged tyranny. The spiritual abuse perpetrated by authoritarian leaders in the Church has resulted in thousands upon thousands of wounded believers—people who can no longer trust the Church to be a sanctuary and who no longer expect pastors to be healers.

In 1978 the whole world watched as a large congregation of naïve souls in Jonestown, Guyana, died because they allowed a madman named Jim Jones to control them with his apocalyptic preaching. In 1993 we watched a similar scenario play out again when cult leader David Koresh and his band of loyal Branch Davidians holed themselves up in a compound in Waco, Texas, and met their deaths, convinced God was on their side and everyone outside their tiny world was deceived.

After watching such tragic scenes on the evening news, many non-Christians are wary of anyone who teaches with an authoritative tone from a Bible. In some charismatic circles, by contrast, *we* are naïve. We put so much trust in our leaders that some of our churches have become virtual personality cults. By our lack of discernment we leave ourselves vulnerable. Many of us, like sheep eager to be led to greener pastures, exercise insufficient caution about whom we follow.

It is time we challenged authoritarianism and called it what it is: an illegitimate use of God's name and authority. It is time we learned to identify illegitimate authority in our ranks, not just to protect ourselves but to spare our friends and family members the pain of spiritual abuse. It is time we cared as much for the flock of God as we do for the reputation of the shepherds. It is time we called for an end to abuse within the walls of our churches.

How can we know when a particular church or church leader is crossing into the danger zone of authoritarianism? Here are seven warning signs I have detected in my own experience:

1. Lack of accountability.

The Scriptures tell us there is safety in the multitude of counselors (Proverbs 11:14). It stands to reason, then, that there is much less safety—perhaps even danger—when a leader does not bother to seek counsel from a wide and diverse group of his or her peers, as well as from gray-haired men and women who have the wisdom that comes with age. If a pastor or church leader is not open to correction from his colleagues, he has set himself up for failure and displayed the most blatant form of pride.

Because the problem of sex abuse by clergy has become such a prominent problem in our society, more and more congregations are insisting that their leaders become accountable to an intimate support group in which they can confess their sins and discuss personal struggles. A humble church leader will admit he needs such a system of accountability. A proud, authoritarian leader will not admit that need, nor dare make himself vulnerable to people he deems spiritually inferior.

2. Lack of acceptance of other denominations, churches or ministries.

The Lone Ranger needs no one to teach him, and his insecurity forces him to compare himself continually with others to prove his superiority. A humble leader, on the other hand, recognizes his limitations and knows he is serving just one function among many in the Body of Christ. Any pastor not in regular fellowship with other Christian leaders in his or her city is sending a clear message: "I have no need of you."

For many years independent kingdom-building has been a typical and acceptable method for ministry in the United States, but it has proven to produce bad fruit. Kingdom-builders end up trying to get some of the glory that belongs only to God. Absolute power, as the saying goes, corrupts absolutely. We need to expect our leaders to display an attitude of humility toward the rest of the Body of Christ.

3. An atmosphere of control.

Authoritarian leaders know how to control people through manipulation. In some cases, this control may simply take the form of subtle suggestions and persuasion. In the most abusive situations, it is applied as threats, legalistic demands, unreasonable requirements and false doctrines. In some cases, especially in charismatic circles, it can come through witchcraft or other forms of spiritual manipulation, like misguided prophecies or "words of knowledge."

Authoritarian church leaders are masters at using Scripture to manipulate people. They often quote 1 Chronicles 16:22: "Do not touch my anointed ones; do my prophets no harm." Another favorite is Hebrews 13:17: "Obey your leaders and submit to their authority. They keep watch over you as men who must give an account." Such passages can be used to intimidate people and keep them from challenging wrong. Some pastors, not recognizing the legitimate distinction between valid criticism and slander, have actually declared that God will curse anyone who criticizes them.

The signs of an oppressive, controlling church environment are apparent. Spiritual heaviness lies like a thick cloud over the congregation, and few believers manifest genuine joy because they are overburdened by feelings of guilt and frustration.

This was the situation with the Galatians. Because these believers had been "bewitched" by Jewish legalists insisting on complicating the Gospel with endless regulations, and because they had begun to follow the dictates of men rather than Christ, Paul told them they had deserted Christ for "a different gospel" (Galatians 1:6); that they were "trying to attain [their] goal by human effort" (3:3); that they must want to be "enslaved . . . all over again" (4:9); and that they had been "alienated from Christ" and had "fallen away from grace" (5:4).

Paul's prescription for recovery from this spiritual ailment is simple: "Stand firm, then, and do not let yourselves be burdened again by a yoke of slavery" (5:1). We are responsible to walk in the freedom provided us by Christ and His Gospel. We must oppose legalism and spiritual control in every form, because to allow ourselves to be controlled is to throw away our liberty in Christ.

4. Dominating attitudes in leaders, usually manifested by haughtiness and anger.

Tyrants are surprisingly similar. Because they want to control their surroundings, they often blow up when people do not conform to their demands or do not conform as quickly as they wish. We expect bullying in the corporate world, but we should not tolerate it among church leaders.

Paul did not tolerate it. He wrote that overseers should not be "violent" or "quarrelsome" but "self-controlled" and "gentle" (1 Timothy 3:2–3). Later he instructed Timothy that the Lord's servant "must not quarrel; instead, he must be kind to everyone" (2 Timothy 2:24).

The Old Testament has plenty to say on this subject as well. Proverbs 22:24–25, for just one example, warns, "Do not make friends with a hot-tempered man, do not associate with one easily angered, or you may learn his ways and get yourself ensnared."

In 1988 a woman who attended an Assemblies of God church in Texas was summoned to the pulpit by the pastor and told that she was a devil. When the woman asked why, the pastor exploded angrily, rushed off the platform and tried to drag her out of the auditorium. One onlooker said the congregation was in shock because they respected the woman for her spirituality.

A few moments later, other members of the church, taking their cue from the pastor, assaulted the woman and prevented her from calling the police. She later reported her plight to a denominational official, and months later filed a lawsuit against the church and pastor. In 1990 she was awarded more than $60,000 in damages for physical injury and emotional pain. The woman's attorney told a newspaper reporter that the jury's decision in the case indicated that "free expression of religion doesn't mean you're free to victimize anyone in the name of religion."

It is sad that such behavior by ministers is not only tolerated but in some cases defended by their followers.

5. Emphasis on leaders hearing God for the people, rather than encouraging them to hear God for themselves.

The Bible teaches that every believer has direct access to God through one mediator, Jesus Christ. Every

Christian, moreover, can hear God's voice personally and expect to receive God's guidance.

In authoritarian church situations, however, members are not encouraged to seek God's guidance themselves. Rather, they are urged to conform to the leader's preferences. In some cases, leaders actually teach their congregations to seek counsel and specific approval from a pastor before making a major decision. Thus, the church members develop an unhealthy dependence on a man in order to function spiritually, and a diminished ability to trust God.

In one charismatic group, pastors encouraged their disciples to check in with them daily to assess their spiritual health and offer any needed guidance. Church members were expected to get approval from their pastors before making major purchases, taking family vacations or planning to have children.

The emotional devastation caused by this kind of perverted control is immeasurable. For many who submitted to the philosophy behind the so-called shepherding movement, it took years to recover from the loss of decision-making ability. They relinquished their wills and lost their backbones—because they viewed absolute obedience to their spiritual leaders as a Christian virtue.

6. Leaders assuming ownership of their people and churches.

Leaders within authoritarian groups operate in a sub-biblical understanding of spiritual authority. Rather than see their role as that of a servant to encourage, strengthen and equip the people of God, authoritarian leaders inflate their own importance and view themselves as somehow "owning" the people God has entrusted to them for spiritual oversight.

In the churches associated with the discipleship movement, for example, it was common for a leader to refer to "his men," meaning the ten or twelve men he was shepherding. This mentality led some leaders to require (though it is hard to believe) that "their men" actually tithe their income directly to them rather than go through a church offering account.

Ownership of the people led to the next step: ownership of the people's resources. In authoritarian environments, pastors often gather to themselves a tightly controlled band of elders (sometimes relatives) to set governmental and financial policies. The church is governed, once again, like a dictatorship, and the congregation has little input into church programs. Pastors' salaries remain undisclosed, and the pastor maintains control of the church board, if there is one. It is, in essence, a form of feudalism that is still accepted by Christians in the twentieth century.

Such a system is a far cry from the biblical view of the church as a living organism, kept vibrant as each member plays a part. All church members should share a sense of ownership in the local church, while realizing that only Christ is the owner of His Kingdom.

7. Women viewed as inferior.

Churches and denominations in America diverge greatly in their view of women in leadership. Some permit the ordination of women, even as senior pastors or bishops, while others maintain that Scripture does not permit women to exercise authority over men in ministry settings.

Apart from these legitimate differences of opinion, it should be noted that authoritarian churches or groups usually discourage women from pursuing any genuine role in ministry. In most of them, women are viewed as important only in their functions as wives and mothers, and they are not encouraged to step beyond these confines to pursue ministry opportunities.

This view creates nothing but frustration, of course. And such a low view leads men to treat women as God-ordained sex objects or drones equipped to perform only menial tasks. Women eager to be used by God or to share their spiritual insights with church leaders are branded rebels or "Jezebels."

The Church was intended to be a place of refuge for the redeemed community, not a place to be browbeaten and abused. How tragic that many of the lambs God has gently prodded into churches associated with the gifts of the Spirit have not found there the loving care of the Great Shepherd.

Serving Ourselves with the Anointing

"Never before has an American evangelist appeared on Soviet state television!"

"No American evangelist has ever conducted such a large crusade in the heart of Moscow!"

"The first-ever Christian meeting held inside the walls of the Kremlin!"

It was a remarkable moment in the history of Christendom when the walls of Communism began to fall in 1989 in the former Soviet Union and the doors of opportunity were flung wide. The collapse of Soviet power signaled a new era for missionary efforts around the world and injected new hope into a Church that had languished under oppression for more than seventy years.

But that golden moment was almost spoiled when opportunistic American evangelicals began to make exaggerated claims about their accomplishments behind the fallen Iron Curtain. Many in the United States winced as we watched our American brothers parading their inflated egos before a culture that had been victimized by egotistical dictators fond of erecting statues of themselves in every park and public square.

One popular charismatic preacher in 1991 mailed a sixteen-page report about his visit to Moscow. The full-color publication included 24 photographs of the evangelist either preaching or standing with his wife in front of the Kremlin. He told his supporters that he had preached "with an anointing of power and authority" to Russian television viewers and thousands of people at a sports stadium. In another sixteen-page tabloid published by the same preacher, his photograph appeared seventeen times. On the cover of one of his books, his image is used five times. Apart from whether this man's ministry is effective around the world, it does seem likely that he has an ego problem.

He is not alone. Many American ministers, driven by a desire to be recognized by their peers, have become a prime target of the demon of egotism. Sadly, they are dragging thousands of Christians along with them.

The head of another ministry in the U.S. attracted thousands to his church, including many from Baptist and Methodist backgrounds who were tired of status quo Christianity. Looking for a fervent faith, they got it in energetic sermons, dynamic worship and multifaceted outreach programs. But following the launching of this preacher's syndicated television program, the Gospel of Jesus Christ began to be overshadowed. A large promotional magazine produced by his ministry in 1990 featured four lengthy articles about his message and divine calling to "motivate humanity." It also included 43 color photographs of him preaching in a third-world country, praying for the sick, hugging supporters, laying his hands on prayer requests, preaching into TV cameras or simply displaying a winsome smile.

We Christians should ask ourselves this question: Has God given ministers the right to use people as a means to satisfy their own egos?

Pride as Spiritual Abuse

What all of us charismatics and Pentecostals must learn is that egotism is a form of spiritual abuse and prostitution—an illegal means to self-gratification at the expense of others. God-fearing church leaders should do whatever necessary to avoid this trap.

The apostle Paul instructed Timothy not to select unproven, spiritually immature men to oversee the church. Such novices, he warned, "may become conceited and fall under the same judgment as the devil" (1 Timothy 3:6). Conceit is a fatal attraction lurking in the shadows of the Church. If unseasoned leaders are allowed to flirt with it, they bring not only condemnation on themselves but havoc on their congregations.

It may seem surprising that in his letter to Timothy, Paul compared egotistical ministers to Satan himself. But Satan's ultimate sin, after all, was pride. Not satisfied to share an exalted place in heaven as an anointed angelic being, he wanted to build his own kingdom. Weary of worshipping God, he wanted worship for himself. And in his pursuit of it, Satan has left behind him a trail of abuse. People are his pawns; he uses them only to get what he wants.

This is also the strategy of the egotistical minister or evangelist. People who show up at services or meetings are useful to help build attendance figures. Parishioners or followers who have money are useful to help fill the collection plate and pay for his TV ministry, expensive foreign car or Italian designer suit. People who think he is God's special messenger will do anything to help him build his own little kingdom.

When we tolerate this kind of ego trip, it leads to more serious forms of abuse like sexual sin and financial mismanagement. Leaders accustomed to using people to satisfy their own egos develop a tolerance for using people in many ways.

This is what happened in part to Jim Bakker and his ministry. The entire PTL empire had been built around the personalities of Jim and his wife, Tammy Faye, and donors were eager to give to support the idea (which turned out to be more of an illusion) that the ministry was making a dramatic difference. But the hype and flashy promotions got so bad that Christian journalist Jamie Buckingham described the Bakkers' TV program as "an hour-long real estate commercial" and "a charismatic version of Romper Room."[1]

PTL donors soon learned that they were being drained of their funds to satisfy Jim Bakker's cravings for acceptance. PTL was a house of cards built on dishonest claims and it came crashing down in 1987. By the time Hurricane Hugo swept through Charlotte, North Carolina, in 1989, damaging more buildings at Bakker's vacant Heritage USA complex, thousands of Christians had come to terms with the fact that they had been used.

Despite Bakker's sexual encounter with former church secretary Jessica Hahn, the PTL fiasco was far more than a sex scandal. Whatever sexual misconduct had occurred inside or outside PTL was only a manifestation of the root problem: an inflated ego and a propensity to abuse. The PTL fiasco, like many scandals in the Church since, was caused by egotism.

Charismatics today are getting tired of kingdom-building and personality-driven ministry. We are less prone to being dragged around to fulfill someone else's so-called "vision." We are more leery of wasting God's money on monuments to the flesh, and weary of being manipulated into being part of someone else's hidden agenda. Some Christians who have been abused in one way or another by egotistical church leaders have been so hurt—and this is the saddest part of the story—that they will have nothing more to do with the established Church. Rather than apply forgiveness in the situation, many have become bitter and refuse to trust Christians altogether.

The only solution is for Christian leaders to make a renewed commitment to biblical humility. Those of us in any leadership role in the Church must stop viewing the people of God as a means to gratify ourselves. We must repent of fleecing the flock and ask God to forgive us for pursuing our own agendas rather than His.

Pride is actually more than abuse; it is insanity. Egotism unchecked actually becomes a form of mental illness—a point colorfully illustrated in the story of King Nebuchadnezzar. The prophet tells us that Nebuchadnezzar lost control of himself after he allowed pride to overtake him:

> He said, "Is not this the great Babylon I have built as the royal residence, by my mighty power and for the glory of my majesty?"
>
> The words were still on his lips when a voice came from heaven, "This is what is decreed for you, King Nebuchadnezzar: Your royal authority has been taken from you. You will be driven away from people and will live with the wild animals; you will eat grass like cattle. Seven times will pass by for you until you acknowledge that the Most High is sovereign over the kingdoms of men and gives them to anyone he wishes."
>
> Immediately what had been said about Nebuchadnezzar was fulfilled. He was driven away from people and ate grass like cattle. His body was drenched with the dew of heaven until his hair grew like the feathers of an eagle and his nails like the claws of a bird.
>
> Daniel 4:30–33

Pride makes human beings crazy. That is what happened to King Nebuchadnezzar. God humbled him by making him lose his mind, and the mighty king learned the hard way that he was the creature after all and not the creator.

Over the years I have watched many charismatic and Pentecostal leaders strut across platforms with a haughtiness similar to Nebuchadnezzar's. They have exulted in their anointing, announced their power over demonic strongholds, threatened to bring God's judgment at their own discretion and used their ostensible spiritual power to manipulate (even intimidate) their audiences. I cringe every time I see this, because I know these men are setting up Christian brothers and sisters for abuse and setting themselves up for a fall.

The Mark of the Beast

A monster called Leviathan is described in the book of Job as a beast so fierce that his crashing caused even the mightiest to fear. This was no ordinary animal, according to the description: "Nothing on earth is his equal—a creature without fear. He looks down on all that are haughty; he is king over all that are proud" (Job 41:33–34).

The creature was apparently one of the fiercest and most dreaded animals ever known. He seemed invincible. His reptilian armor was impenetrable. When he finally surfaced to breathe, his huge frame, usually hidden under the ocean depths, was horrible to behold. This monster was a master of terror:

"Who can strip off his outer coat?
Who would approach him with a bridle?
Who dares open the doors of his mouth,

ringed about with his fearsome teeth? . . .
Strength resides in his neck;
dismay goes before him. . . .
The sword that reaches him has no effect,
nor does the spear or the dart or the javelin.
Iron he treats like straw
and bronze like rotten wood. . . .
A club seems to him but a piece of straw;
he laughs at the rattling of the lance."

Job 41:13–14, 22, 26–27, 29

Leviathan no longer lives on the earth.[2] Changes in the earth's climate after the flood of Noah's day probably drove the creature to extinction. But the spirit of Leviathan lives on. This invincible animal who terrorized humanity but was finally wiped out by God represents the spirit of pride, the force that inflates human egos to lofty proportions and tempts us to live as if we were self-sufficient.

There is no question that in American society the spirit of Leviathan flourishes. We have become a nation of success addicts and overachievers . Winning is everything. The business world emphasizes the biggest, the best, the hottest and the fastest, enticing America to an endless pursuit of first place. The healthy competition that stimulates a free economy has given way to an incessant striving to achieve, regardless of moral principles or the cost to others.

Sadly, the pride of Leviathan is equally evident in many of our churches. We have been marked by the beast. We are gripped by a spirit of self-promotion. Church growth has become less a matter of winning individual souls to Christ than an impersonal numbers game. We have become proud, self-sufficient and insensitive to people's needs.

This spirit of pride is manifested in three ways:

1. A lack of servanthood.

Jesus told His disciples that they should call no one either *father* or *teacher* (Matthew 23:9–10). He also explained to them that the Christian idea of leadership is contrary to the pagan concept. "Whoever wants to become great among you," He told them, "must be your servant, and whoever wants to be first must be your slave—just as the Son of Man did not come to be served, but to serve, and to give his life as a ransom for many" (Matthew 20:26–28).

The Christian concept of leadership conflicts with the accepted ideas of Western culture. Servanthood is not the American way. We like the concept of the rugged individual who pulls himself up by his bootstraps. We make gods of our heroes. Like the ancient Greeks, from whom we borrowed so much of our current thought, we still worship the image of the god-man. Adonis, Apollo and Aphrodite are still competing in the Superdome, performing in Hollywood or topping the Fortune 500 listing.

Much of the New Testament was written to address the superstar syndrome. Paul hammered continually on the theme that the Kingdom of God is composed of many inter-dependent members. We all have different functions but we all need each other. The teenager who picks up the trash after the worship service is as important as the most talented speaker.

But because the pagan idea of leadership pervades our churches, many of us are in constant pursuit of celebrity status in the Kingdom of God. Rather than seek the favor of God, we seek the recognition of others. We prefer to rule than to serve. We are driven not because we want to meet the needs of others, but because we want to be admired by them. We are settling for success in the eyes of men rather than a heavenly reward.

2. An overemphasis on personal greatness.

The American Church has heard plenty of teaching in recent years about personal destiny, reminding us that God has a calling on every person to accomplish a specific task in His Kingdom. Most of this has been beneficial; but we must take care that our teaching about destiny does not degenerate into a lust for greatness. We must constantly place our desires for recognition (or power or fame) on the altar. Even Christian ministry can become an idol in our lives and keep us from being used by the Holy Spirit.

Paul exhorted us to have the attitude that was in Jesus Christ: "Do nothing out of selfish ambition or vain conceit, but in humility consider others better than yourselves. Each of you should look not only to your own interests, but also to the interests of others" (Philippians 2:3–4).

Jesus was tempted, before He began His ministry, to accomplish His mission Satan's way. He could have proclaimed Himself the ruler of all the kingdoms of the world, and Satan would have granted Him more honor and fame than any earthly king has ever known. But Jesus rejected the devil's method to greatness. The path He chose to walk was one of humility, self-denial and obscurity. He would die virtually unknown.

Jesus told His followers they must follow the same path. To seek our *own* life, He said—to pursue advancement, promotion or fame in the eyes of others—is to forfeit fruitfulness in His Kingdom. A seed, before it can produce anything, must die in the ground.

All of us in the charismatic renewal need a swift return to these simple truths of self-denial. We need to learn humility. Rather than emphasize the need to fulfill our own destinies, those of us in any form of ministry need to view our primary calling as that of equipping others to achieve their full potential.

3. Competition within churches and among Christian leaders.

Paul also said about Jesus that He came to earth in the form of a bondservant, and that He "did not consider equality with God something to be grasped" (Philippians 2:6). Grasping for power and position among charismatic and Pentecostal leaders, by contrast, has become commonplace.

Walls of isolation and division have been fortified between and even within denominations as leaders compete for the title of biggest and best. Rather than link arms to achieve a common goal, we have pursued the largest congregations, the nicest buildings, the biggest mailing lists, the most television time. In our zeal to "kick in the gates of hell" and "stay on the cutting edge," we have lost sight of the humble nature of our Leader.

Our Western philosophy, so steeped in competitive tradition, has done plenty to squelch true fellowship and love in our churches. Leaders find it hard to express genuine affection for one another. Pastors stand aloof from their congregations and from each other because this subtle competitive spirit prevents a sincere expression of brotherhood. And the Holy Spirit is prevented from moving among us in this restrictive atmosphere.

Happily, there is increasing cooperation among certain Christian ministries and churches that we did not see even ten years ago. Pentecostals who have typically been isolationist are working with other evangelicals. Parachurch ministries like Youth With A Mission and Campus Crusade for Christ are cooperating with denominations. "Partnering" has become the new buzzword in the missions community.

When a coach meets with a group of athletes in the locker room just prior to the last game of the championship, he motivates them with a go-out-there-and-tear-'em-up pep talk. But that was not the scene that occurred when Jesus spent His last evening with His disciples. We are told that He laid aside His garments, dressed like a servant with a single towel around His waist and washed the feet of His friends.

Then He gave them this charge: "Now that I, your Lord and Teacher, have washed your feet, you also should wash one another's feet. I have set you an example that you should do as I have done for you" (John 13:14–15). Jesus did not call the disciples together in a huddle and incite them to compete for first place. Rather, He demonstrated to them that the battle would be won only through mutual love, covenant, cooperation and transparent relationships.

If charismatics and Pentecostals set servanthood, humility and mutual cooperation as our goals, we would see fruitfulness on a scale we could hardly now imagine.

Bracing for the Storm

he book of Acts begins with the Holy Spirit falling on the early Church on the Day of Pentecost amid "a sound like the blowing of a violent wind" (Acts 2:2); and it ends (as we saw in chapter 3) with Paul caught in the middle of a violent windstorm. It fascinates me that one of the last events recorded in the Bible is a shipwreck. It is a perfect prophetic message from a first-century historian alerting us that spreading the Gospel is fraught with challenges. Let's look at this prophetic message in greater detail.

After proclaiming the Gospel to King Agrippa in Caesarea, Paul was bound in chains and put on a ship bound for Rome, so he could appeal to Caesar. Bad weather plagued the voyage from the beginning. By the time the crew arrived near the coast of Crete, having ignored a warning from Paul that "our voyage is going to be disastrous" (Acts 27:10), Luke the historian tells us that a violent northeaster hit:

> The ship was caught by the storm and could not head into the wind; so we gave way to it and were driven along. As we passed to the lee of a small island called Cauda, we were hardly able to make the lifeboat secure. When

the men had hoisted it aboard, they passed ropes under
the ship itself to hold it together. Fearing that they would
run aground on the sandbars of Syrtis, they lowered the
sea anchor and let the ship be driven along.

We took such a violent battering from the storm that
the next day they began to throw the cargo overboard.
On the third day, they threw the ship's tackle overboard
with their own hands. When neither sun nor stars appeared for many days and the storm continued raging,
we finally gave up all hope of being saved.

verses 15–20

We do not have to spiritualize Paul's last recorded
missionary journey. It is a detailed account of a har-
rowing sea voyage. But behind Luke's matter-of-fact report of a boat being tossed from Caesarea to Crete to
southern Italy, we can draw some insights that will help
us understand how the Holy Spirit works today. But first
listen to the turning point of the story:

After the men had gone a long time without food, Paul
stood up before them and said: "Men, you should have
taken my advice not to sail from Crete; then you would
have spared yourselves this damage and loss. But now
I urge you to keep up your courage, because not one of
you will be lost; only the ship will be destroyed. Last
night an angel of the God whose I am and whom I serve
stood beside me and said, 'Do not be afraid, Paul. You
must stand trial before Caesar; and God has graciously
given you the lives of all who sail with you.' So keep up
your courage, men, for I have faith in God that it will
happen just as he told me."

verses 21–25

The clear message of Acts 27 is that God called Paul
to stand before Caesar and that no storm would stop

that from happening. The Gospel would be preached to the whole world, just as Jesus prophesied before His death (Matthew 24:14). Paul trusted God against terrible odds, in the midst of a deadly tempest, and his faith saw him through.

But there is a subtler message in this passage that we should heed. Perhaps Luke's vivid account of a shipwreck concluding his narrative known as the Acts of the Apostles serves as a warning—that those following the leading of the Holy Spirit and seeking to further the purposes of God will face treacherous waters. Unless we choose to follow Him fully, listening carefully for His voice, we ourselves may experience *spiritual* shipwreck.

When the crew aboard Paul's ship realized the severity of the storm, they threw excess baggage overboard. On the third day they dumped even the ship's tackle into the sea—the gear necessary for raising and lowering the weights of rigging—in an attempt to save their lives. Finally, when they had abandoned all hope of being saved, Paul prophesied that while the ship would be lost, all the crew would arrive safely ashore. His word proved accurate: Their vessel broke up into a thousand scattered boards but the crew washed up safely onto the beach at Malta.

Those of us who identify with the charismatic renewal find ourselves in the midst of a perilous storm, clinging for dear life to our own wind-tossed vessels. We want desperately to reach our destination, and God has promised we will arrive there safely. But He does not promise that our vessels will. In fact, some of our structures are about to break up beneath us and be swept away. We are faced today with a critical choice: hoist our extra baggage overboard or go down with it. As the storm increases in intensity, as I am sure it will, our extra baggage will become less and less important to us. We will eventually let go of it.

For several years we have watched as dozens of prominent charismatic ministers have perished in this storm.
Ministries with million-dollar budgets have been re-
duced to bankruptcy and shame. Prominent leaders who
tried to hide their sin from God have been humiliated
publicly on network news programs. Some who used the
anointing of the Holy Spirit as a means of personal gain
have been exposed. But amid all these dramatic ship-
wrecks, Jesus Christ continues to move His Church toward her final destination. Those ministries and
churches that have kept their focus on Him and viewed
the gifts of the Holy Spirit as a means to evangelize the
world and build up believers are not sinking beneath
the waves. Like the apostle Paul headed in determina-
tion toward Rome, they have a divine mission to fulfill.

Five Ways We Can Respond

Mission researcher David Barrett estimated in 1990
(in the table displayed in chapter 2) that there are nearly
92 million so-called "post-charismatics" in the world—
people he defines, in relation to the charismatic renewal,
as "irregular, or less active, or annually active, or for-
merly active, or inactive, or elsewhere active."[1] Some of
these post-charismatics, once identified with charismatic or Pentecostal groups, have returned to non-
charismatic churches because of disillusionment or some
other problem, or abandoned their faith altogether. This
huge number of post-charismatics does not negate the
fact that Pentecostal and charismatic churches are growing faster than any other Protestant or Catholic group
in the world. But we cannot ignore the fact that large
numbers of charismatics leave our ranks every year.

I know why some of them leave, because I know some
of them. They have been abused by authoritarian church

leaders; or they have become disillusioned because they trusted in some doctrine (like the idea that God will always heal if we activate enough faith); or they have witnessed a gross misuse of the gift of prophecy; or they have been wounded by a proud pastor or painful church split that left them mistrusting authority figures; or they have stopped participating in the life of *any* local church because an egotistical pastor with a self-serving agenda turned them against organized religion.

The natural reaction to any of these hurts is to throw out the baby with the bath water. But there is a better alternative. Rather than watch our wounded brothers and sisters turn their backs on the faith or reject genuine spiritual experiences, those of us who identify with the charismatic renewal should determine to help rid our movement of its extra baggage. Let's renounce what is counterfeit (fabricating the anointing) and start hoisting each of the other problems overboard that we have also discussed in this book—our egotism, authoritarianism, materialism, mysticism, elitism and separatism. I recommend we start doing this in five specific ways:

1. We must return to our original focus.

When the charismatic renewal broke out in America's mainline churches in the 1960s and '70s, the experience shared by clergy and laity alike was simple. We were celebrating the vibrant reality of Jesus Christ Himself as we experienced the everyday movings of His Spirit. We were learning to enjoy worship, thrilling over the joys of answered prayer and sharing our faith with others. Even though we found a new understanding of the Person of the Holy Spirit, we presented the call to be baptized in the Spirit as a means to receive more of Christ and to be empowered to share His message with others. We were not departing from the message of the Gospel; we were rediscovering it.

But it did not take long for that Spirit-born fervor to be replaced with fleshly hype and enthusiasm. Within a few years many charismatics had "graduated" from simple truths. We began to focus on peripheral doctrines that served no purpose other than dividing the Church into a thousand charismatic sub-groups.

The same scenario occurred in first-century Corinth. We know from Paul's first letter to that congregation that those believers had received *all* the gifts of the Spirit (1 Corinthians 1:7) and witnessed the miraculous power of God. But he complained in his second letter that they had departed from their original level of spiritual fervency:

> I am afraid that just as Eve was deceived by the serpent's cunning, your minds may somehow be led astray from your sincere and pure devotion to Christ. For if someone comes to you and preaches a Jesus other than the Jesus we preached, or if you receive a different spirit from the one you received, or a different gospel from the one you accepted, you put up with it easily enough.
>
> 2 Corinthians 11:3–4

This passage makes it clear that the devil delights in diverting our attention from Christ. His method, Paul indicates, is to use spiritual decoys—counterfeits that look and sound enough like God to deceive us. Many such counterfeits have become part of charismatic church life today in America. Like the Corinthians, we bear with this beautifully. The Living Bible says it better: "You swallow it all."

During the early days of charismatic renewal in the U.S., it seemed that God had opened up a supernatural spring to flow freely through churches that had been dead spiritually for decades. Like the Children of Israel in the wilderness, we had sudden access to a stream of clear water gushing from a rock. But when we allowed our focus to turn from Christ to peripheral issues, that stream became polluted. Our streams in the U.S. are so polluted today, I fear, that few can find spiritual refreshment.

Paul told the Corinthians they had embraced another Jesus, another Spirit and another gospel. Let's ask ourselves: Can unbelievers who visit our Sunday morning services encounter the living Jesus? Or is the Jesus we preach some bizarre aberration, a Jesus whose primary interest is in giving us goose bumps or luxury cars? Can unbelievers who visit our churches find the Holy Spirit? Or do they find nothing more than a charismatic show, full of theatrics but devoid of spiritual substance? Do they find the Gospel or a nuts-and-bolts exhortation on how to grow a congregation to the mega-church level?

We charismatics tend to think that as long as our church services are "exciting," meaning full of loud praise music and motivational sermons, sinners will find Jesus when they happen to wander in. In reality, it might be just as hard for those sinners to find Christ in our churches as it would be to find Christ amid the cold formality of a mainline denominational church where the pastor reads weekly excerpts from *Psychology Today*.

Only God can make our polluted stream pure again, but we must ask the Head of the Church to refocus our attention on Him. Jesus told His disciples before His arrest that the Holy Spirit would not glorify Himself when He came. "When he, the Spirit of truth, comes," said Jesus, "he will guide you into all truth. He will not speak on his own; he will speak only what he hears, and he will tell you what is yet to come. He will bring glory to me by taking from what is mine and making it known to you" (John 16:13–14).

In some instances, I dare say, we charismatics have elevated the Holy Spirit to make doctrinal points or prove doctrinal arguments. But the Spirit did not come to elevate Himself; He was sent to glorify Christ. In all our emphasis on the Holy Spirit's ministry and gifts and power, let's be careful to magnify the One the Spirit came to magnify.

2. We must develop a healthy skepticism.

Charismatics have a reputation of being gullible. Since we believe in the supernatural, we are sometimes suckers for any bizarre thing that comes along. Nor are we famous for asking hard questions. In fact, many charismatics view any kind of questioning as a sign of weak faith or even rebellion.

But healthy skepticism is a biblical virtue. Any thinking Christian concerned about the welfare of the Church will not let a minister's questionable remark go unchallenged. And a wise, discerning Christian who cares about the honor of God's name will not swallow some bizarre "revelation" without checking it first against the revealed will of God as recorded in the Bible.

Sadly, even though we are vocal proponents of the nine gifts of the Spirit, we demonstrate too seldom the gift of discernment. The root of our problem is not, I believe, a lack of discernment, but a warped view of spiritual authority. Many of us have been taught that laymen should under no circumstances question church leaders or point out their faults. In many charismatic churches, this teaching gives leaders an almost cult-like control over their congregations. But if they are saying, "Don't ask questions; God will take care of me if I get out of line," even if we go along with it, they have no scriptural leg to stand on.

The apostle John, on the contrary, urged the early Church to ask tough questions. "Dear friends, do not believe every spirit," he told them, "but test the spirits to see whether they are from God, because many false prophets have gone out into the world" (1 John 4:1). Pastors and church leaders who want their parishioners to develop godly character and maturity would never discourage honest inquiry.

Obviously God has ordained orderly government in His Church, and encouraging healthy skepticism does not give church members license to challenge their pastor's every move or order him around. But for the most part, charismatic churches tend to be more beset by problems rooted in authoritarianism than in unbalanced congregational rule.

I am not suggesting we all become heresy hunters, looking for false doctrines under every bush. But we must get rid of our naiveté. We must accept the fact that Satan is a deceiver and that he uses people—false prophets—to divert our attention from Jesus. And we must learn to discern the difference between a true message from God and a counterfeit.

Several years ago, when I was working for a news organization in Washington, D.C., I learned that a certain Oklahoma businessman was conducting Christian ministry activities in Israel. Although on the surface his work sounded legitimate, I felt troubled about it. Something did not seem right, and I have learned that we should pay attention to this kind of internal disturbance. Often it is the Holy Spirit's gift of discernment.

As I looked into the matter further and made some telephone calls, I discovered that the man had served time in prison for promoting a fraudulent investment scheme. Now it appeared that he was ready to do it again, only this time his target audience consisted of gullible Christians. I contacted him, asked for an interview and was stonewalled. So we published a story raising questions about his activities and informing our readers of his criminal record.

In 1992 a self-proclaimed "Christian accounting expert" began advertising his seminars on church law and financial management in major evangelical magazines. He billed himself as a virtual savior, promising he could save churches thousands of dollars in taxes if they would heed his advice. But within a few months, complaints about the man began to circulate among Christian legal groups. Churches were receiving exorbitant bills for bogus accounting services and some were given false information about tax requirements.

Then a Texas newspaper revealed that this so-called authority on money matters was a con artist who had lied repeatedly in his advertisements and seminars about his educational background and qualifications as a tax consultant. Despite the newspaper report, however, the man was still operating his business and drawing crowds to Christian seminars in mid-1993.

We would all rather not think about the fact that con artists prey on God's people. But we must not ignore it. The Church will be a safer place when we get serious about exercising godly discernment.

3. We must pursue unity with other evangelicals.

One of the most visible byproducts of the charismatic renewal has been an unprecedented level of unity among Christians from varied denominational backgrounds. The baptism in the Spirit is a common denominator linking believers who have seldom associated with one another. Lutherans, Presbyterians, Baptists, Methodists, Episcopalians, Mennonites, Catholics and old-line Pentecostals have realized they are part of one diverse Body—a cause for celebration.

But we have continued, amid our bridge-building, to fortify our walls. For the most part we charismatics operate within our own comfortable confines. We speak our own language complete with buzzwords. We utilize our own prayer methods. We promote our own practices, some of which are not modeled in Scripture. We have, in fact, become isolationists. Our attitude toward non-charismatic brothers and sisters can be one of indifference: "We don't need them and they don't need us, so why should we try to work together?" Non-charismatics wish charismatics would stop being so loud, juvenile and theologically sloppy, while charismatics wish non-charismatics would stop being so stuffy, rigid and spiritually cold.

But these attitudes are precisely what Paul condemned in his classic discourse on Christian unity: "There are many parts, but one body. The eye cannot say to the hand, 'I don't need you!' And the head cannot say to the feet, 'I don't need you!'" (1 Corinthians 12:20–21).

Granted, there are major doctrinal issues at stake in this dispute. Many non-charismatics—fundamentalist Baptists, for example—are vehemently opposed to any suggestion that the gifts of the Holy Spirit are operational today. They have themselves become isolationist, adopting the view of charismatics that "we don't need you." But in many ways we have been just as rigid and doctrinaire as our fundamentalist brethren. (Reactions to the John MacArthur book *Charismatic Chaos* are just one example.)

There are indications, however, that rigidity on both sides may be softening. In 1989 Joe Aldrich, president of Multnomah School of the Bible, began leading four-day interdenominational prayer summits for pastors in the Pacific Northwest. Aldrich, who does not wear the charismatic label, started the prayer meetings simply because he was burdened about the pitiful spiritual condition he saw in the states of Washington and Oregon.

Acting on the theory that genuine revival can be ignited only after church leaders have been "renewed and retooled," Aldrich organized the first pastors' prayer gathering in 1989 near Salem, Oregon. It was not a typical ministerial meeting. The men traveled to a remote spot on the Pacific coast to pray, worship and fellowship for four days. Leaders representing Baptist, Episcopal, Evangelical Free, Presbyterian, Methodist, Lutheran and various charismatic and Pentecostal churches united to form a rare mixture of styles, tastes and doctrines. Denominational differences were ignored while prayer, brotherly affection and the worship of Christ were emphasized. The rule of thumb guiding the meetings, Aldrich said, was simply "No agenda."

Ron Boehme, a Youth With A Mission leader from Seattle who participated in a prayer retreat in Kitsap County, Washington, in 1990, said he was especially moved by the way leaders voluntarily set aside their denominational barriers. At one point, he said, an Assemblies of God minister stood to his feet, tears flowing, to announce that he was guilty of judging a conservative Baptist colleague in the room.

"I was told in Bible school that you believed all the wrong things," the Pentecostal pastor confessed. "I thought you were elitist."

"I thought the same about you," the Baptist replied. "Would you forgive me?"

The two pastors embraced and shed more tears together.

Terry Dirks, who works with Aldrich at Northwest Renewal Ministries, said that in one prayer gathering a Lutheran pastor stopped prayers to admit that he could not continue without repenting for criticizing charismatics from his pulpit. His candid apology prompted a remorseful charismatic pastor across the room to renounce a smug attitude he normally vented toward non-charismatics.

"I've been judgmental," the charismatic pastor responded. "I'm no better than you. To think that I'm blessed more than you is a mockery of God's love for all of us."

By mid-1993, 94 of these prayer summits had taken place in seven states and three Canadian provinces with the participation of thousands of pastors. I suspect they foreshadow the direction the entire American Church will be taking in the next few years. Church leaders on both sides of the charismatic aisle are sensing that God wants us to overcome our petty divisions.

God will not allow charismatics to claim the credit for sparking spiritual revival in America, any more than He will share His glory with any man or woman. We must pitch overboard our elitism, our holier-than-thou attitudes and our doctrinal divisions.

4. We must demand standards of accountability for church leaders.

There is no question that Americans in the 1990s are revolting against all forms of institutional corruption. We were enraged in 1992 when we learned that U.S. congressmen and congresswomen were allowed to bounce checks at taxpayer expense at the federally run House of Representatives bank. We were appalled to learn that same year that the head of the United Way, one of America's most respected charities, was profiting personally from the generous donations of middle America. We were disgusted when we learned that some American doctors were performing unnecessary medical procedures on elderly patients in order to collect Medicare funds.

But many charismatics and Pentecostals were defensive (though Americans in general were disgusted) to learn that men of God like Jim Bakker and Jimmy

Swaggart—men who preached biblical holiness—were living according to a sub-biblical code of ethics.

One does not have to be a prophet to predict that in the next few years the leaders of the Church in America will face the anger of the people in the pews. In 1993 the Roman Catholic Church was hit hard by this rage, as people faced the tragedy of child sexual abuse by priests, covered up (and therefore allowed to continue) by the institutional Church. Protestants are ready to stage their own revolt against corruption in church leadership. And charismatic churches will definitely be affected, too.

Our tolerance level has reached a new low. We are finally beginning to demand accountability in church finances to prevent pastors and ministry leaders from accumulating wealth and power. We are beginning to insist that any church- or ministry-sponsored fund-raising be carried out without a hint of manipulation or coercion. We are stipulating that clergy abide by the same moral standards that Scripture requires of every believer.

A group of women in suburban Atlanta might be a harbinger of things to come. They began a crusade in 1993 to pass legislation that would make clergy sex abuse a criminal offense in the state of Georgia. The women had been members of Chapel Hill Harvester Church, and (although the church officially denied the charges) each claimed she had been sexually harassed or violated in some way by Chapel Hill pastors. Tragically, these women felt they had no recourse but to go to the secular media and a state lawmaker to find a listening ear. Many of them said they had tried repeatedly to resolve the conflict by talking with church leaders, but were rebuffed each time or told to work out their problems with the men involved.

The situation at Chapel Hill revealed to many of us that we have no workable system in place to deal with serious morals charges. The independent nature of many charismatic churches makes it impossible to impose discipline. So a minister accused of sexual impropriety can simply deny the charge and state from the pulpit that the accuser is an instrument of Satan. He can then continue in his ministry, the issue unresolved.

Because no group of church leaders stepped into the Chapel Hill situation to conduct an ecclesiastical trial, the matter was simply dropped. Within a few months it was business as usual at the church. Those who claimed to have suffered abuse joined other churches and were often told simply to put the matter behind them.

I suspect the way this situation was handled is more common than we think among independent charismatic congregations. In many churches, an authoritarian leadership structure has set pastors up as almost unapproachable. They sometimes project the attitude that they are infallible. If such a pastor falls morally or embezzles money from a church account, his sin can easily be swept under a rug.

Recently a charismatic leader who had been charged with serious sexual improprieties attended a conference hosted by another prominent pastor. At one point in a worship service, the pastor called the man out of the audience and "prophesied" to him that God would cause his accusers to come to him and apologize for what they had said. The pastor was assuring this man, in effect, that he had done no wrong. He concluded by saying, "Thus says the Lord."

This prophecy exemplifies the lawlessness that rules much of our movement today. Sin can be covered up with a wave of the hand from a prominent leader. Pastors can engage in whatever behavior they slip into and find immunity from any penalty. They may divorce their wives, marry their secretaries and speak at the next big charismatic convention within a year. And if anyone questions their behavior, they assure their followers that they have been singled out by the devil for spiritual attack because of their unusual anointing.

It is time we called for an end to this Lone Ranger style of church government. We must demand standards. We must stop providing financial support to ministers who refuse to make themselves accountable.

5. We must not support kingdoms centered around a human being.

One of the greatest temptations facing men and women is the desire to build our own kingdom. We spent the last chapter looking at the problem of egotism—serving ourselves with the anointing. This is illustrated in the story of the Tower of Babel, when the residents of Shinar conspired to construct a monument to themselves that would reach into heaven.

Men and women today are still building their lofty towers. Political leaders, corporate executives, Hollywood producers and media moguls are busy erecting imposing structures to display their importance to the world. And sadly, the spirit of Babel is at work within the religious world as well. Christian men and women can fall into the trap of building structures that are fashioned in their own image and for their own purposes.

God will have the final say, of course, about which structures will remain standing after His judgment. The apostle Paul wrote that each person must take care how he builds: "No one can lay any foundation other than the one already laid, which is Jesus Christ" (1 Corinthians 3:11). Structures built out of wood, hay and stubble, as we observed in chapter 8, will be burned up in the fire of God's holiness.

No one can say how much of what is being built today will stand God's test of fire. But we can be assured that any ministry serving someone's ego will be the first to go up in flames. Any church aiming to impress the community rather than please God will not endure the heat.

In 1993, after relocating to a new city, my wife and I began an earnest search for a church home. Because we had belonged to several different churches, denominational ties meant little to us. We were as comfortable in an Episcopal church as we were in a Pentecostal or Baptist congregation, so long as we sensed the presence of the Lord there. As we visited churches, we began to discuss what we were looking for in a church home. We had likes and dislikes, of course, and wanted our children to feel welcome in the Sunday school. But for the most part we were open to a wide variety of options. We knew God had a specific place for us, however imperfect it might be, that we could call home. But as our search continued, I sensed one clear directive from Him: *Don't join a church that has a manmade agenda.*

Many of our churches today have adopted manmade agendas, and lost their commitment to follow the Holy Spirit and help establish the Kingdom of God. Some churches are simply complying with a denominational agenda that may be ten, twenty, even fifty years old and irrelevant to today's culture. Some pastors may be building an audience around their pulpits or airing a TV broadcast to impress their ministry colleagues. And too many churches in America have one all-important agenda item: Grow to be big. In congregations where mega-ministry is the goal, people often are herded into services, counted and fed just enough Scripture to keep them committed tithers so that the 5,000-seat sanctuary can be paid for.

I do not mean to suggest that large churches cannot be in the perfect will of God or that the goal of reaching more people is not godly. But during the 1990s I suspect we will do a lot of reevaluating as to what the Church is all about.

God is finished with the one-man show. Ministries centered around an individual cannot meet the spiritual needs of God's people or make a lasting impact on our communities. In coming days I suspect we will see less emphasis on the role of professional clergy and more emphasis on casual, lay-driven ministry. God has given church leaders a task, according to Ephesians 4:12, "to prepare God's people for works of service." Leaders are servants of the Church, not lords or taskmasters. They have been called to fulfill Christ's grand agenda, not their own.

....

Throughout this book I have offered what some readers might see as a gloomy picture of the spiritual condition of the charismatic renewal movement. I have talked about the poison of elitism, the dangers of mysticism, the sin of separatism. I have issued warnings about false prophets, religious con artists and Lone Ranger apostles. And I have suggested that this movement that has stirred the American Church since the turn of the century has been a breeding ground for deception.

But I have not given up hope, and I am certainly not writing off the charismatic renewal. Even as I write, the stirrings of a neo-Pentecostal movement are being felt in some of the nation's largest black denominations— churches that were not open to the charismatic renewal before. The largest church in the National Baptist Convention, for example, 7,000-member Greater St. Stephen's Full Gospel Baptist in New Orleans, is now a fully charismatic congregation where the baptism in the Holy Spirit is taught from the pulpit. Astute observers of the black church scene say the transformation of Greater St. Stephen's may signal the beginnings of a new renewal movement that could reshape the African-American religious landscape.

Other beacons of hope shine within our movement. Some of America's largest and most innovative churches are identified with the charismatic renewal, and many of them are challenging racial barriers and breaking new ground in difficult urban areas. In fact, charismatic churches in the U.S. have led the way in beginning to integrate Sunday morning worship, though much remains to be done.

And the renewal is helping transform our world. In South Africa, a charismatic church led the way toward the dismantling of the official government ideology behind apartheid. Charismatic churches in East Germany have been credited with laying the groundwork for the fall of the Berlin Wall in 1989. Pentecostal churches in Latin America are helping to promote the principles of democracy and religious equality.

Sure, we have our problems. We are carrying around plenty of excess baggage that needs to be pitched overboard. (We do *not* pitch at our peril.) But none of our sins or excesses is too big for God to handle. We must simply be honest about our defects. If we can weather the coming storms and allow God, through the Holy Spirit, to purge us, we will see a glorious Church emerge, one "without stain or wrinkle or any other blemish" (Ephesians 5:27).

I believe we will find that our best days are yet to come.

Notes

Chapter 2

1. Barbara Reynolds, "Religion Is Greatest Story Ever Missed," *USA Today*, March 16, 1990, p. 13A.
2. David Aikman, "The American Media: Still Avoiding the Story of the Century," *The Forerunner*, January-February 1988, p. 12.
3. Interview with George Otis, cited in "New Missions Strategies for a Rapidly Changing World," *National & International Religion Report*, January 28, 1991, p. 3.
4. Vinson Synan, *Launching the Decade of Evangelization* (South Bend, Ind.: North American Renewal Service Committee, 1990), p. 56.
5. David B. Barrett, "The Twentieth-Century Pentecostal/Charismatic Renewal in the Holy Spirit, with Its Goal of World Evangelization," *International Bulletin of Missionary Research*, July 1988.
6. Barrett, Annual Statistical Table on Global Missions: 1993, *International Bulletin of Missionary*

Research, January 1993. Definitions of categories are explained in *World Christian Encyclopedia* (1982); see also *Our Globe and How to Reach It: Seeing the World Evangelized by* A.D. *2000 and Beyond* by D. B. Barrett and T. M. Johnson (Birmingham, Ala.: New Hope, 1990).

7. Barrett, "The Twentieth-Century Pentecostal/Charismatic Renewal in the Holy Spirit, with Its Goal of World Evangelization," reprinted from *International Bulletin of Missionary Research*, July 1988.

8. Francis MacNutt, Christian Healing Ministries, Inc., Vol. 5, Issue 5, p. 1.

Chapter 3

1. Rodney Lensch, "God's Perestroika," *Rod and Staff* newsletter, November 1989.
2. D. R. McConnell, *A Different Gospel* (Peabody, Mass.: Hendrickson Publishers, 1988), p. xvi.

Chapter 4

1. John MacArthur, *Charismatic Chaos* (Grand Rapids: Zondervan, 1992), p. 83.
2. Ibid., p. 46.
3. Ibid., pp. 202–203.

Chapter 5

1. Quoted by Steven Lawson in "The Foursquare Church Faces the 21st Century," *Charisma*, March 1993, p. 26.
2. Dennis and Rita Bennett, *The Holy Spirit and You* (Plainfield, N.J.: Logos, 1971), p.77.

Chapter 7

1. The so-called cessationist view is accepted doctrine in many evangelical churches. It states that miracles, prophecy, speaking in tongues and other gifts of the Spirit ceased after the age of the early apostles. Proponents of this view hang much of their case on 1 Corinthians 13:10, in which Paul says the gifts will pass away "when perfection comes." Cessationists insist that "perfection" refers to the New Testament, implying that the gifts of the Spirit were no longer necessary after Christians gained access to the complete Bible.
2. Wark, Andrew, "Like Sheep without Shepherds: The Threat of Heresy in the Chinese House Church Movement," News Network International, July 21, 1992: pp. 4, 7.
3. Ernest Gruen, et al., *Documentation of the Aberrant Practices and Teachings of Kansas City Fellowship (Grace Ministries)* (Shawnee, Kan.: Full Faith Church of Love, 1990), p. 149.
4. Ibid., p. 89.
5. Ibid., p. 139.
6. John Wimber, letter from the National Board and Council of the Association of Vineyard Churches (Anaheim, Calif.: November 7, 1991).

Chapter 8

1. Francis MacNutt, *Overcome by the Spirit* (Grand Rapids: Chosen Books, 1990), p. 73.

Chapter 9

1. Jim Bakker, letter dated June 20, 1992, mailed by Tammy Sue Chapman, New Covenant Church, Largo, Fla.

Chapter 10

1. "Mumford Explains Why," *Ministries Today,* January/February 1990, p. 52.
2. Ibid., p. 55.

Chapter 11

1. Jamie Buckingham, "God Is Shaking His Church," *Charisma*, June 1987, p. 21.
2. Leviathan is also mentioned in Psalm 74:14, Psalm 104:26 and Isaiah 27:1. Although some scholars have suggested that this animal was a crocodile, hippopotamus or whale, many creation scientists believe he was an aquatic dinosaur. Leviathan is often translated *sea monster.*

Chapter 12

1. Stanley M. Burgess and Gary B. McGee, eds., *Dictionary of Pentecostal and Charismatic Movements* (Grand Rapids: Zondervan, 1988), p. 826.